Praise for *Empathy Works*

"With an engaging style, thoughtful research, and wisdom, Sophie Wade articulates the most critical skill of great leaders and companies—how they listen to, empathize with, and react to their employees and customers. A highly recommended read for leaders and aspirational leaders of tomorrow."

NORMAN DE GREVE, CMO, CVS Health

"The bar continues to rise for more inclusive workplaces, and empathy is a trait and practice all leaders need to have in their portfolio, today. Based on her many years of experience advising organizations, Sophie Wade understands this and provides valuable insight here into making the case for empathy in business and the benefits it can bring to organizations of all sizes."

KARYN TWARONITE, a global leader in Diversity, Equity & Inclusiveness

"The past two years have broken all the conventions of work and *Empathy Works* makes a convincing case for reframing all aspects of corporate life to make it work more effectively for people and the heart of a company's strategy."

MARK READ, CEO, WPP

"The assumption that individuals turn up for just a paycheck is clearly outdated. Our expectations of work and the value of work have changed—and it's not just about Gen Z. Increasingly we all expect to see the diversity of our own experiences understood and reflected in our company's culture, including work practices that allow for more flexibility and celebrate inclusivity. *Empathy Works* is an essential guide to developing one of the most critical leadership tools in the modern workplace. Transactional conversations that focus on the job at hand may seem time efficient, but as Sophie Wade illustrates, through a series of case studies and exercises, building empathy with colleagues and customers is key to establishing trust, unlocking creativity, and is an important source of competitive advantage."

PAULETTE ROWE, CEO, Integrated and E-commerce Solutions, the Paysafe Group

Empathy Works

The Key to Competitive
Advantage in the
New Era of Work

Empathy
Works

A. SOPHIE WADE

●●
PAGE TWO

Cataloguing in publication information is available from Library and Archives Canada.
ISBN 978-1-77458-151-3 (paperback)
ISBN 978-1-77458-152-0 (ebook)
ISBN 978-1-77458-153-7 (audiobook)

Page Two
pagetwo.com

Edited by Kendra Ward
Copyedited by Jenny Govier
Proofread by Alison Strobel
Cover design by Peter Cocking
Interior design by Fiona Lee
Interior illustrations by Jonathan Brown
Printed and bound in Canada by Friesens
Distributed in Canada by Raincoast Books
Distributed in the US and internationally by Macmillan

22 23 24 25 26   5 4 3 2 1

sophiewade.com
empathyworks.online

To Liam & Gigi
You inspire me to be a better person and mother.
This book is for you. It is my impassioned contribution
to more positive and productive working lives.
With much love.

Contents

Introduction

I T WAS after dinner, at the end of a multi-day conference for business owners in 2018, and I was chatting with another woman at my table, Jenn, the Founder and CEO of a book-keeping and consulting firm.

"I simply cannot fill three new associate-level positions," Jenn told me. "Hiring new associates has been getting harder each year, but now my business is actually threatened by my inability to recruit the people I need."

I understood her dilemma. The accounting/book-keeping sector is one of the fields where digitalization has already been replacing many entry-level tasks and even some entire jobs. I could imagine that younger folks, aware of these trends, would be less likely to look for a job—or even consider a career—in this industry. They would have valid reason to be concerned their job might be automated away.

Jenn and I discussed the long-term problem and a potential strategy of liaising with local colleges to connect with, pitch, and convince future graduates. However, that would not address her immediate needs. We dug deeper to look for other solutions.

"My company is very customer-oriented," Jenn said. "Account executives are on-site at client locations for every meeting to review documents and input data. We have always differentiated ourselves from our competition with our personal touch."

"What if your consultants used video conferencing for client meetings? That would free up their time for other clients by saving the commuting to and from each location. Documents could be shared electronically and reviewed together with clients online. Questions could be asked before the associate inputs the data. It doesn't solve the hiring problem, but it would optimize your current employees' time while you look for more candidates."

Jenn shook her head. "That won't work. Our commitment is to keeping our customers' businesses alive, and a key way we do this is through our dedicated on-site service and support."

This founder is a tough cookie. She has been running her own business for more than twenty years while raising four kids. We had already had a lively—and productive—discussion two years before about workplace flexibility. I cared about finding a way for her company to get through this tough patch.

We went back and forth again and again. I proposed more ideas—schedules, logistical arrangements, and shared resources—that might ease or resolve the current issue.

"That won't work," Jenn said.

I explained that updating technologically was the future of her industry, and any tasks or jobs at risk would be absorbed in the process. Candidate reticence about obsolescence could then be put to rest.

"No, that won't work," she said again.

Jenn was adamant. After more than half an hour of proposing solutions to no avail, I was feeling desperate. She was determined to maintain her setup, which, she said, helped her clients stay in business—and that was her immutable commitment.

That is when I had an epiphany: I had been empathizing with Jenn and trying to fix *her* problem, while she was empathizing with her clients and trying to ensure *their* needs continued to be met. My mistake. I reframed the message.

"How about you position the video conferencing application as *how* you serve your clients. Upgrading how you service them, adopting new technology, is *how* you help them adapt for the future and enable them to stay in business?"

Jenn stopped. She said nothing. This time, my approach was aligned with how she saw the world and the clients' issues she was sensitized to.

I held my breath. I might have found the message and delivery that worked. It was the same proposition that I had mentioned at the beginning of our talk; however, now I had explained it as an experience Jenn's clients could benefit from, rather than as a convenient solution to deal with a staffing problem that should not affect her clients.

Within three months, Jenn hired a Millennial with technical skills who helped her develop a digital strategy for the company and upgrade to use video conferencing to service her clients much more efficiently. Shifting her approach to how she fulfilled her commitment demonstrated a mindset that understands that future iterations may require altering the model, methodology, or means of delivery, while upholding the same quality of service.

We both benefited from our interaction. Personally, I learned much more about extending my empathetic understanding. I did not fully recognize until sometime afterwards that there had been a significant disconnect at the beginning of our discussion, when I did not realize how deeply Jenn empathizes with her clients. Because of her dedicated attention to their issues and tapping into what they were going through, Jenn interpreted my suggestions—which were geared to addressing *her* problems—as discordant with her strategic orientation. So long as I did not relate any potential solutions to her *clients'* experiences and how they would be taken care of, my words would fall on deaf ears. And they had! I could have short-circuited some frustrating moments if I had empathized with Jenn's consideration of her clients' situations and presented sooner how technology-based options would work for *all* parties, especially her clients.

From my perspective, the positive outcomes were also the important steps Jenn took to support sustainable growth for her business:

- Reviewing business processes with a long-term strategic perspective while staying true to her dedicated customer focus, commitments, and connections

- Hiring someone with a relevant perspective and skills to develop and implement appropriate digital tools for her associates to serve her clients effectively

- Integrating operational flexibility to adjust for ongoing changes in the business climate, including a smaller local talent pool

- Upgrading the digital strategy and infrastructure that allows her to attract new associates who realize the company has the vision to succeed and grow

From that moment on, Jenn was much better prepared for the Future of Work, with its interwoven emphasis on technology and talent.

The Future of Work

What is—or *was*—the Future of Work? There are many definitions out there, but the key elements describe our new, digitized, data-driven, interconnected, faster-evolving, globally integrated business environment. The fundamentals are significantly different from previous operating parameters, such that we need comprehensive shifts in our mindsets, methods, and operations to be adaptive and responsive enough for inherent, ongoing iterations and mini-pivots. It is exciting, daunting, challenging.

The new environment, this new era of work, expands possibilities and creates extraordinary opportunities, as well as challenges conventional means, methods, and practices. Between 1976 and 2012 the employment share of routine occupations decreased from 60 percent to 40 percent, while non-routine occupations—including projects of different sizes, increasing teamwork in changing combinations, and varying objectives and timeframes—experienced significant growth.[1] The content, form, and format of much work is different as well—we are doing more knowledge than machine work, exercising more collaborative human ingenuity supported by algorithmic processing than oversight of brute machine force.

The Future of Work, our new work environment, is also human-centric. A tectonic shift has been happening as technology stops defining our lives and starts putting people—as consumers and workers—front and center. Technology now provides us with cutting-edge services and tools that enable us to choose how we want to live and work.

A linchpin moment happened in our personal lives in 2009, when the developer platform of the early iPhones opened up and third-party applications exploded. With powerful mobile computers in hand, we could now access an extraordinary array of options: entertainment events, retail experiences, health-care support, travel opportunities, weather information, and much more besides. As customers, we were empowered.

We started demanding more customized communications rather than blunt blanket advertising delivering generic messages. New technologies provided sophisticated means to synthesize intelligence gathered from wide-ranging activities to identify and reach us individually, as consumers and businesses. We began to want, and expect, highly targeted channels to find us, know us, and serve us each tailored offerings.

For us as employees, the impact of technology has also been significant, with a plethora of tools enhancing our capacities and capabilities, facilitating sales, improving marketing reach, gathering data, streamlining project management, adapting operations, and much more. Human Resources (HR) technologies have been proliferating, with increasingly sophisticated applications and customized services for workers, such as personalized benefits options. Moreover, with dramatic effect on our working dynamics, processes, and experiences, machines no longer dictate where and when we must be at work. There are individualizable alternatives. Technology has empowered, and is no longer tethering, talent.

As leaders and managers, are we surprised employees are echoing our customers' demands—looking for more customized communications, personalized services, individualized accommodations? As consumers, customers, and coworkers, we have been yearning and pushing to experience more of the benefits that technology affords us.

Wait, what? Who is ready for empowered and untethered talent? Confined to the office or locked down at home, it was mentally manageable. But let loose and liberated?! What now? We know ourselves and how far we might want to go, yet we are also aware that our own marketplace demands have raised the bar—outside and in—for the businesses we work for.

But do we know what our customers really want? We need to connect with, serve, and respond to our customers better and faster. To do that, we need our employees to step up their game. But how is that done? How can we discover what our employees need to lean in and engage, to embrace new business parameters and solve new problems? And, to do that, do we need to meet their new demands?

Empathy is the skill that enables us to understand and relate to each other, customers and employees alike, in

- outreach to prospects, to connect with their pain points;

- relationships with customers, to strengthen bonds and open up sharing conversations;

- innovation and product development, to elevate user-centric design-thinking;

- leadership roles, to motivate, guide, and support each direct report to do their best work;

- employee exchanges, to listen, learn, and facilitate productive teamwork;

- operational functions, to engage employees to be responsive to conditions and each other;

- vendor and partner discussions, to ensure alignment and flexibility along the supply chain; and

- consistent and effective people-focused interactions throughout our business ecosystem.

As the first emphasis of your business, empathy works in powerful ways to help you connect with buyers. Empathy works to align, integrate, and maximize the efforts of your extended talent pool oriented towards achievement of your business goals. With empathy, you cultivate a strong, cohesive culture that can uphold your business and workers going forwards.

In fact, empathy is a founding value that influences our behaviors and actions. Empathy is a mindset and a lens through which to orient how our businesses run. Empathy helps us understand each other, create an inclusive environment, bring open minds, communicate clearly, collaborate well, resolve conflict more easily, connect across geographies, lean into difficult conversations, create safe spaces, adapt to changes together, and support each other. Empathy is also an essential skill that informs and guides our interactions.

Empathy rose in prominence in my work—interacting with large and small groups of corporate executives, software users, salespeople, technologists, and marketers—as I heard the struggles, stresses, and complaints of CEOs, HR leaders, and frontline managers. They had three interrelated priority issues driven by the changes catalyzed by technology:

- Traditional leadership styles were becoming much less effective.

- Demands from younger employees were discordant and disruptive.

- Using conventional management methods with distributed individuals and teams was ineffective.

These issues were all about relating to others as human beings, and they all pointed to empathy—listening to feedback, hearing concerns, observing reactions, and understanding needs. Synthesizing external inputs as well as numerous documented research studies, I became conscious of empathy's strategic role as we transition to very different, digitized working environments. As we each individually integrate and practice empathy, we improve our effectiveness, growth, and success, and that of any organization we work for or with.

Starting in 2018, clients picked up on my empathy solutions, asking me to highlight empathy as the headline, rather than the secret sauce. I got more and more requests to do keynotes and workshops, consult, and write on empathy at work. I have four online video courses focused on empathy that well over 450,000 people had taken as of January 2022. As we moved inexorably towards the Future of Work, empathy became increasingly important, appearing with more frequency in my writing and integrated into the applied "how" of successful working practices. Empathy was the clear solution: for executives, managers, and employees to understand each other better; for new styles of leadership, or "leading from within"; for bridging generational communications gaps; and for optimizing management and performance of distributed teams.

This book describes the empathetic guiding orientation for the Future of Work, or—more appropriately—a new era, the new "now" and "how" of work. Empathy generates the human counterbalance to technologically driven environments.

The "Now" and "How" of Work

As the framing, substance, and realities of our work change and our attitudes and approaches evolve in tandem, empathy becomes strategically important. Part I of this book describes the "why," "why now," and "how" of empathy—which provides a stronger foundation for our working lives, as a core value, mindset, and skill to practice. Part II explores and explains how empathy is integral to navigating today's evolving business and work environments—still working through the multidimensional impact of the pandemic—and the shift to a more human orientation in our professional customer- and employee-centric dealings. Part III puts principles into practice, showing how and where to prioritize empathy and the habits to integrate into your work routines to improve relationships, responses, and results.

Throughout, I have included quotes and stories from numerous interviews I conducted in 2020 and 2021 with clients and other business leaders in small and large companies around the world—spanning the United States, Europe, the United Kingdom, and Australia. Many interviews were originally for my podcast *Transforming Work with Sophie Wade*, which I launched in February 2020 to help people navigate the changing workplace, anticipating the advent of the Future of Work that then arrived in a rush. I am deeply grateful to everyone who generously shared their insights and experiences during, and looking beyond, the pandemic.

By reading this book, you will have a greater understanding of what empathy is and why it matters. You will learn how to practice empathy to find, attract, and convert customers more easily, as well as lead, engage, motivate, and retain your employees. You will find out how empathy helps you work effectively in teams across all kinds of projects dealing with complex and unexpected challenges. You will find out how to encourage and cultivate empathetic mindsets and habits in others around you.

However your business generates revenues, integrating empathy strategically throughout its ecosystem increases conversion rates and operational effectiveness and improves customer and employee experiences. Empathy works to give you a critical founding value. Empathy works to give you a coherent approach and operating principles. Empathy works to give you a consistent approach to create new, human-centric rules of engagement and work practices so that your digitally enhanced company grows successfully and sustainably.

Read on and you will gain a useful understanding of what the Future of Work is all about now that it is here. Read on and you will become versed in the high-level and core elements of the new business environment and what these mean for your company, customers, and workforce. Read on and you may be comforted to learn that we have been anticipating the multidimensional issues confronting us *for years*, and we do know how to act and advance—with empathy.

PART I

THE WHY, NOW, AND HOW OF EMPATHY

Empathy is the ability to put yourself in someone else's shoes and feel what they are feeling.

1

Why Now?

THESE ARE liminal times. We are in the throes of transformation—a period of change that is both exciting and challenging. The old rules of engagement are out of date. Some rules have been thrown out, new ones are being drafted and tested, and others are still being revised. That's fine; it's time.

The old rules were not absolute. They were defined, not divine—written by human beings just like us. The old rules were thoughtful and determinative, based on previously gathered and synthesized collective knowledge and experience. They utilized the (very limited) datasets and understanding they had *at that time*. Previous generations wrote those rules for *their* prevailing conditions—enabled and constrained by the crude available technology, organizational hierarchies, industrial infrastructure, and societal norms of the time. They aimed to support the needs and expectations of the local and regional markets they served.

Now, our needs and expectations of work are very different. Our ecosystems have expanded globally; the pace of market developments has increased, driven by sophisticated, interconnected technologies, and accelerated by the COVID-19 pandemic; and organizational structures have flexed and flattened in accommodation. Through continued uncertainties, we are working more closely together in teams, on projects, and across silos, for which we need more cohesive corporate culture and communities and to lean heavily on our interpersonal skills, especially empathy.

Your Role and Responsibility

The good and the bad news is that *you* are now participating in crafting the new rules. As our social contract is re-examined and reworked, you might not have the time or inclination to influence the overarching framework and landscape by contributing to general debates across industries. But the shifting parameters and attitudes, the unbundling of jobs, the repacking and reconfiguring of work, and the increasing emphasis on skills are affecting us all. And the changes are ongoing.

In your local setting, however, your participation in developing new rules is a given. Your business will not be equipped to keep moving forwards and achieve sustainable growth without conscious and considered updating of the terms upon which your business engages, throughout its ecosystem. What are the new means and metrics for identifying prospects, attracting buyers, serving customers, interacting with vendors and partners, and treating your total talent pool? You have already been working on different aspects. However, bringing a purposeful, broad, and strategic—rather than tactical—approach will serve you best for the long-term to create a coherent framework that aligns all necessary elements.

You must have a comprehensive understanding of where we are. You will benefit if you purposefully look at the big picture and develop new ground rules relevant for understanding the significance of this period of adjustment to what was named the "Future of Work"—our "now" of work. Our new, digitally enhanced reality.

I can imagine you want to influence, steer, and determine the evolving parameters of your business, which means recognizing the interdependencies, themes, and threads throughout your ecosystem. In crafting, drafting, and testing new guidelines, you become all the more aware of marketplace dynamics and can adjust and respond to future developments, as well as nurture the foundation and essential skills for your organization.

The Wave of Transformation

I would like to nerd out for a moment and retreat up to 50,000 feet. I must tip my hat with great reverence to the phenomenal futurist, the late Alvin Toffler. His books *Future Shock* and *The Third Wave*, published in 1970 and 1980, respectively, describe his visions, which were extraordinarily insightful, long-term predictions, projecting the trends he was observing around him at the time.

I will describe a few particular elements of his clairvoyant wisdoms in a nutshell. Such brevity hardly does his work credit, but it allows us to appreciate the essential logic that informed his invaluable prognostications and explain what we are currently dealing with. It is then easier to realize where we are and why, and how empathy plays an inevitable, strategic role as we move forwards.

Technology advances first brought us the Industrial Revolution—the Second Wave, as Toffler describes it—with its enormous electromechanical machines that transformed our agrarian lives, delivering millions upon millions of identical products.[1] Manufacturing was accomplished in factories by production lines of massive, connected machines. Efficiency required scale, and bigger became better to attract the capital required to invest in equipment. Leaders controlled these corporate behemoths, governed by six interrelated principles: standardization, (mass) specialization, synchronization, concentration, maximization, and centralization.[2]

In what Toffler defined as the Third Wave, further technological developments allowed for smaller and more capable machines, such as desktop computers, followed by mobile laptops and even smaller and more powerful smartphones. Size and price reductions led to greater proliferation, more varied uses, and drove what Toffler called *de-massification* of production, media, society, and work.[3] We are increasingly able to focus market segmentation and cater to smaller and smaller audiences. This has affected how we market, distribute, sell, run operations, work, and live.

The de-massifying transformations started rocking people's lives in the 1950s, but they have been accelerating since around 2007—with the advent of the smartphone. It has now been more than half a century since the shift started, and advances have been compounding, but with uneven distribution and impact, which is perhaps why, looking back, the turbulence created by the pandemic felt much like a tsunami. As if at the seafront in 2020, we saw the bedrock of our businesses and work models exposed as lockdowns pulled back the protective layers. We recognized what support was there, or not, and for whom. As the accelerated wave of change crashed down upon us, we could see some of the harsh realities of who would be impacted most by what was ahead.

COVID-19 Chaos

The COVID-19 pandemic struck with a vengeance in March 2020. From one week to the next, our situations—work, lives, and relationships—were changed almost beyond recognition. Our familiar, comfortable contexts were dramatically altered. As we were shaken with fear about a new, deadly, and highly transmissible virus, we were thrown into a confusing chaos of uncertainty. How would we live? How would we work?

Luckily, we had no idea yet what extraordinary and prolonged tragedy and turmoil lay ahead. We were able to focus near-term to rally, pivot, and adjust our lives and work practices as much as we could to stay safe and keep going. We hunkered down at home or sprayed and sanitized, washed and wrapped up in protective gear.

Frontline workers were subject to severe stress in crisis mode round the clock that extended to weeks in repeated waves. They had no downtime to relieve their mental strain and vent their grief. Those working from home, often isolated or overcrowded, were now squinting at colleagues on-screen, trying to figure out how to handle tasks from decentralized settings. They were also trying to stay connected with family and friends from afar whom they could sense were scared or stunned and needing support—just as they themselves were. We all were.

Throughout our lives and around the world, empathy went into overdrive. We leaned in for each other. Dispersed family generations sought to bridge geographic distances, technical savvy, and emotional dissonance. Managers struggled to respond to their fragmented teams, in charged mental states, who needed them to provide more individualized attention, empathetic understanding, and support than they were used to or ready for. Using their empathy skills, leaders who could read personal cues and recognize burnout situations could take appropriate action and better assist and sustain their team members through the crisis, wherever they were working. We became much more aware of our human depth—especially the pain, grief, mental stress, and suffering. More empathy was needed and noticed.

With video windows into one another's situations, we learned more depth and dimension about our colleagues and clients. Emotionally vulnerable ourselves, we developed heightened awareness towards coworkers and became more sensitized to what they were going through. From day to day and week to week, emotions could swing—sometimes dramatically—because of family pressures, health issues, or pandemic worries, with additional major stressors relating to racial injustice and discrimination.

We learned much more about ourselves: how and when we work well and do not, what matters and does not, and how we can innovate to satisfy our needs as much as possible. We got creative when captive! Innovations ranged from practical to entertaining to surprising, from facial temperature scans to six-foot-long social distanced coolers, and from virtual show-rooms to remotely shot commercials.

Crisis as Catalyst

Meanwhile, businesses were rushing to implement new distributed platforms, integrate new applications, and adapt workflow—often barely defined—to the extent that was viable at that time. Executives had to keep their businesses going while swiftly evaluating what operations were relevant to continue based on snap assessments of how customers might react in the weeks ahead. They were attempting to empathize with people's experiences, forecast their possible new behaviors, and discern how to fulfill changing requirements.

Operational infrastructure was morphing, constrained by the pandemic as behavior shifted to online interactions for information exchange, communication, and commerce, supplemented by careful contactless payments and curb-side pickups. These extensive, expanding human and digital networks were mutually reinforcing as they became more integrated, catalyzing the crisis-driven, accelerated arrival of the Future of Work in 2020.

This was a *huge* deal. However, it went mostly unreported and unremarked as viral waves, tragedies, politics, vaccine development, and economic hardship dominated consciousness around the world. Prior to 2020, heralded and resisted, applauded and ignored, the Future of Work had seemed far enough away that most people put off dealing with it. The urgency was not there. Suddenly, just as we were reeling from crisis conditions, there was a silent, seismic shift.

Masked by the pandemic, the underlying fundamentals of many developed economies were reaching more highly connected and digitized levels, spurring further real-time data sharing and technology-facilitated, intelligent capabilities. The impact of the COVID-19 crisis on the "Internet of Things" was a growth in projected market size from US$150 billion in 2019 to US$243 billion in 2021—a compound annual growth rate of 13.7 percent.[4] Networked data conduits are expanding and extending further daily.

Even as the COVID-19 crisis caused waves of turmoil, digitized market transactions and data feedback were moving incrementally faster. As restrictions continued, consumers' changing access, sentiment, and habits buffeted organizations trying to find and convert hesitant prospects into customers and upsell nervous clients or find completely new ones. The severely challenged and unpredictable business climate motivated executives, marketers, and salespeople to identify and forecast the most likely potential buyers for updated iterations or additional products and services. Under pressure, people rallied to sell, and to keep businesses operating and people employed—collaborating across departments, stepping across business lines, even reallocating people to different roles.

Muriel Clauson, Co-founder of Anthill, which creates talent mapping software for deskless workers, was surprised by some executives' unexpectedly rapid shift in mindset. She said they were navigating change with their people, exploring, "What if people don't actually have a job in our company? What if people are part of teams that work on different tasks? We are actually leveraging their experience, knowledge, and interests in real time, where it's needed in the company."[5]

Exploratory projects were less straightforward, having to be handled across newly decentralized teams, requiring greater cross-functional cooperation to hasten responsiveness. Video conferencing "made the ability to reach people in other functions easier because you didn't have to walk into that department," observed Robert Birge, Chief Growth Officer of global online fashion retailer ASOS.[6] Video communications bridged office-based physical and invisible barriers between divisions, and standardized video windows reduced hierarchical layers. We rallied, we learned, we adapted; we leaped forwards or pivoted in a new direction.

Pandemic Possibilities

All these activities compounded pre-pandemic Future-of-Work trends that organizations had been struggling to adjust to. Emergency conditions then caused many entrenched rules to be adapted as normalcy evaporated. Barriers to working across silos without integrated budgets dissolved. Resistance faded to interdisciplinary cooperation to test new products and services.

The crisis threw all the chips up in the air, pushed us far beyond our comfort zones, and freed us up to get really creative as we necessarily focused on what mattered work-wise—

finding viable solutions to keep our businesses going by think-ing *way* outside the box. At the same time, the new speed, connectivity, and data accessibility, enabled by recently inte-grated technologies, disrupted the manual and mechanical constructs and constraints of our pre-pandemic existences, enabling us to adapt to and make habitual new digitized, boundaryless, integrated interactions. This was the Future of Work in action, heralding our new era.

The multidimensional disturbance to our lives and clash of our personal and professional environments generated a rare period of inflection. Crisis conditions presented an extraordinary opportunity for each of us to take stock of life at forced distance or during intense frontline stress. With conventional rules initially on hold and then increasingly under review, we did not just glimpse, we *experienced* that our working lives could—and perhaps "should"—be very dif-ferent. Questions have been proliferating as we reassemble and resettle. During this state of flux, your company needs to transform fully for the new realities of your ecosystem and create meaningful competitive advantage with a sustainable way forwards.

Maybe you understood and worked with, not against, some of the changes around you as the pandemic raged on, recognizing new and enduring characteristics. Perhaps you sought to absorb and learn from new work models that could also provide flexibility for variant-generated restric-tions, contingency plans, and tech-driven Future-of-Work requirements. Or you may have been more focused on driv-ing through the chaos, dealing with immediate deadlines. If you did not absorb the long-term nature of the changes and realize you *can* forecast ahead, it is understandable. Although, projecting earlier trends, work futurists have long anticipated these conditions, scenarios, solutions, and viable responses.

Restoring Order

Reinstating rigid office-based constraints on people's working lives could not provide the desired benefits in those entities where executives rushed to restore order as we had known it before. Forced to relocate to mostly unfamiliar home/work settings in 2020, how much more aware did you become of the pros and cons of restrictive work environments? Any employees recalled back to the office were sensitized to compare the limitations of being allowed only one work location. Swapping one set of limitations for another was problematic when new non-office-based settings became valid options and people finally recognized that constraints that undermine motivation and engagement reduce their productivity and creativity. We all saw stats such as the Harris Poll in August 2021 that showed only 37 percent of US employees wanted to return to working full-time in the office.[7]

We hope the worst of the pandemic's disruption is behind us, although COVID-19 is mutating and sticking around. Hiccups will occur and remind us to keep contingency plans in our virtual top drawers, so that people are prepared and business operations can adapt. But, whether working within a physical corporate structure that is partly or wholly distributed, the changes wrought by the Future of Work's arrival will continue to create havoc until leaders finally recognize and absorb its transformative impact. A new era of work has begun.

Creating new, inflexible experiences is not the type of order that benefits your business—which continues to operate in unpredictable, but more stable, conditions. You were right. Regressing—trying to move forwards while simultaneously looking back over your shoulder—could not get you where you want to go. Our energy is best applied to creating order without the rigidity of previous structures, taking a progressive track forwards.

Have you remarked how you have acclimated and adapted already? Have you noticed how you are absorbing almost real-time new market intelligence? Have you registered how you have created new habits: assessing the relative importance of data, incorporating more information into weekly reports, and adding detail to product or service sales, marketing, and development updates? Implicitly or explicitly, your organization is developing its new long-term, more adaptive strategic framework and operating practices.

Transforming Work

At the same time, challenging market conditions put new pressure on businesses to be creative and innovative. Consumers' and companies' behaviors are changing, including those of your customers. Have you felt the increased stress on yourself and your team members? New business orientation needs to incorporate operating practices and new ways of working that support pivots and people, that embed technology and empower talent. Moreover, one of the pandemic's lasting effects is our memories of feeling burned out by the constraints, isolation, overwhelm, and blurred working and living conditions. We understand the importance of social contact better. We yearn for stability and security. We want options, having finally realized how our rigid work schedules and settings had long been undermining and limiting performance.

However, the necessary, progressive way forwards, embracing new optionality, is not just about offering employees more location and scheduling choices. The changes go much deeper and wider than that. We need to recognize employees as individual human beings—which is why we need to integrate empathy as the essential value, mindset, and skill into our working and operating practices.

We are at a different place now. The ground is not solid, but it is stable. Since the Future of Work arrived, the marketplace looks different. We have new working environments, about which there is much existing understanding. We know how to adapt for current conditions. We are not flailing in the dark. We can work out what foundation we need and what skills to use. We can gather the data and identify what we have learned. We can craft the future deliberately, strategically, thoughtfully. We must bring new, open mindsets, as old, fixed approaches are insufficient. For now, we must keep iterating on plans that try, test, and build on the best of what we have done, absorbing *recent* insights and understanding so we can adapt, move forwards, and be successful.

The options, settings, and requirements are sufficiently different such that we must significantly revise the rules of engagement that have governed our leadership styles, influenced our mindsets, dictated our approaches, and determined the social contract. Under current conditions, new leadership dynamics, rules, and operating practices are necessary, *and* we have more understanding about what motivates people and supports strong performance.

This is the moment to review recent data and reflect, to project new pathways and generate a new orientation, strategic framework, and guidelines for your organization and ecosystem. This is the moment to use research and relevant insights to cultivate a cohesive and supportive environment by nurturing your company's culture and community. This is the moment to recognize, understand, and act upon people's perspectives and experiences—your prospects, customers, and blended workforce of employees and contractors. This is the moment to make changes that matter, adding meaning, dimension, and flexibility to the working lives of people at your company.

Empathy Takeaways

- We are in a period of transformation. Previous operating rules are no longer valid; we must participate in defining and developing new rules of engagement.

- The COVID-19 pandemic caused such extraordinary disruption that it created a unique opportunity to reconfigure our businesses and working lives.

- Implementing digital platforms and applications during the COVID-19 crisis accelerated the arrival of the Future of Work, forever changing our operating and work environments.

- The progressive track that embraces new, flexible frameworks and updated operating rules is the viable way forwards for a sustainable path of growth.

2

Why Empathy?

"IF YOU don't feel well in a place, you don't want to go there," said Matthias Hollwich, Founder at HWKN, a global architectural innovation firm. "Office buildings need to become aspirational—where people want to be and feel that they belong."[1]

I was intrigued. Matthias always integrates a deeply empathetic understanding of human beings into his building designs.

"I researched *unforgettability*," he said, describing how he developed his vision for the future of office buildings. "An unforgettable city started out with a sculptural element. Then I realized unforgettability also comes from the people using it and people engaging with each other." Matthias integrates concepts from his work on resorts, where guests are guided along a trajectory that connects them by means of social encounters and activities, and the resort operator participates in the experience.

He took me through his new concept, which he calls "Resorting": The employee's journey starts by traversing an external neighborhood environment, picking up coffee and first connecting with colleagues, with music or inspirational content to support their transition before they arrive at a welcome desk, not a lobby. After "moments of delight," they can partake in a "moment of efficiency," perched at a work bar to do emails, before transitioning to office space, called a "Work Villa," for a group meeting. Or they may find a "Work Cabin" for a one-on-one space, or access lounge areas for relaxation, or balconies for inside/outside work environments.

Matthias showed me inspirational as well as more subtle versions of office designs that emphasize employees' experiences—their emotional journeys and energy levels—throughout their workdays, to help them do their best work. He said, "We need to create buildings that become the social connector again and a corporate culture communicator by inviting people to come in, but not forcing them to come in. The office becomes a place where people want to be, which is designed incorporating essential elements of team identity and community building. An offering that the company entices you to use."

Matthias's vision incorporates the fundamental concept of this book: that people matter. Not just in a warm and friendly way. They all—we all—matter as an essential and strategic emphasis for our businesses. Human-centricity is the core organizing principle for creating meaningful connections and engaging experiences with people within our organizations and throughout our ecosystems. A consistent and comprehensive people-focus enables your company to create competitive advantage and achieve sustainable growth in the more complex and rapidly evolving landscape that characterizes the new era of work.

Our working environment—our corporate culture—is fundamental, wherever our precise work locations. The culture is the foundational platform that we build upon, and the values it encompasses influence our actions. Empathy is an integral value to highlight within your company's culture to guide human-focused behaviors that we now lean into and learn from. When we practice and act with empathy, we emphasize the people within our ecosystems.

Historically, we have been transactional in our interactions and management methods, perhaps mimicking our treatment of the machines that have been central to our economic development for decades. Reams of data exploring human motivation and engagement have illustrated that people's experiences ultimately drive their decisions, dedication, and determination. Now, sufficient advancements and a catastrophic crisis have accelerated our integration and relegation of technologies to their appropriate roles as critical tools that we can all utilize to achieve our objectives.

Dealing with more complex, relationship-based business situations, empathy is the skill that empowers you in any communication to or with another person—nearby or at a distance—with multidimensional insights about their thinking and experience. Empathy is the core competency of emotional intelligence, which encompasses complex relationship management skills such as managing emotions, influencing and mentoring people, and teamwork. Practicing empathy, you develop a more comprehensive understanding of any situation so that you can make informed decisions about how to act, whether you are involved in selling, marketing, connecting, communicating, collaborating, creating, managing, or motivating someone. No matter if you are dealing with a customer, prospect, partner, colleague, direct report, family member, friend, or even a stranger on the street, empathizing informs and improves your interactions with them.

Externally Focused Empathy

How can we successfully attract, sell, and convert—never mind produce for—a target market of one if we do not understand what they really want and why?

In decades past, advertising to huge TV audiences meant blasting faceless crowds of millions. Bold but bland messages could only hope to generate common feelings of excitement or happiness, share general knowledge, stimulate broad curiosity, create overall awareness or—best-case scenario— establish small foundational blocks on which trust in a brand might be built. It was, and is, simply not possible to relate to a vast population's myriad points of view and their experiences when trying to convince and convert them individually into customers.

Not so now. Our narrowed focus enabled by technology has resulted in strategic marketing exercises that include describing and serving sample *singular* customer profiles. In our de-massified market, targets can be modeled as individual people whom we might actually recognize in the street, connect with, and relate to. We need to use our interpersonal skills more to be sufficiently equipped not just to imagine our potential buyers and current customers, but also to understand them with enough depth to create what they really want or need. This is all the more taxing considering the distracting state of flux around us, which can certainly cloud people's clarity.

We need to get prospects' attention as they seek to make thoughtful progress while they are simultaneously debating: *Should we be continuing in this direction? Do we need to review parameters, since our clients have modified their habits? What will help us achieve our goals? I want to live somewhere else, so how can I negotiate with my boss to go fully remote?* We can certainly empathize with their confusion and challenges as we are all in similar situations.

Amidst ongoing market shifting, we need to intersect with people and companies and clearly convey the compelling fit of our carefully tailored product or service, based on their specific scenarios and pain points. The most effective way to achieve this is by developing empathetic awareness and understanding of them, and by building trusting relationships so that they share more details with us. We can then hone our offerings to meet their voiced and discovered needs, and can explain the fit convincingly. Satya Nadella, CEO of Microsoft, emphasizes empathy frequently, saying in 2017, "If I look at what is Microsoft's core business, it is about being able to meet the unmet and unarticulated needs of customers and there is no way we are going to be able to succeed in doing that if we don't have that deep sense of empathy."[2]

As the spotlight shines down on each individual, the bar has been raised. Product development specialists have been pioneers leading the charge in designing for identifiable users and figuring out their real needs. Empathetic design-thinking, perspective-taking, deep listening, observation, and connecting with personal sensibilities has enlightened us about end users' actual habits, pain points, and issues.

Communications Cycles

How can we compete without highly targeted, responsive messaging?

Your marketing department, working together with web developers on the e-commerce side, may already create some empathy-informed decision trees that potential buyers self-select. Highly personalized customer journeys are based on the researched or revealed preferences of users who navigate sophisticated interface designs that incorporate a detailed empathetic reading of users and an exploration of their experiences. The result is a rapidly flowing loop of data that you are no doubt very aware of, as its importance has risen. You gather, analyze, and act upon that data in order to remain competitive and ensure your business offerings stay relevant and evolve along with customers' needs and changing outlook. Coordination of communications is also needed, to match the current consumer sentiment and to create the desired interest or action, using empathy skills to do so.

Cycling into the market through numerous parallel and interconnected communication channels are a variety of carefully selected, tightly honed, and informative calls-to-action. These messages and images are digitally coordinated and coded to reach specific targets—who have been identified with psychographics—from multiple angles. However, have you checked the optimal frequency of updating marketing copy after surveying converted customers and interested leads? Timing may vary until market conditions are more stable. Regular discussions are worthwhile, so that easy opportunities are not missed and leads are cultivated.

And customers are talking back too! Cycling back to the company, incoming data capture the opinions of activated customers who are now easily able—and more willing—to express and share their (dis)satisfaction widely. Have you already seen what happens when communications about your offerings are poorly crafted or inauthentic and not tuned in to what potential customers are actually envisaging or how they are feeling? Have you had to deal yet with new clients' feelings as they experience your service rather than what was promoted and promised, if their reactions were assumed rather than empathized with, then tested and verified?

Gaps between new buyers' expectations and their post-purchase realities are likely to result in noticeable reactions from the marketplace that call out—usually negative—discrepancies. Jumping in quickly to fill in these disconnects is most effective when employees with well-exercised empathy skills play a key role in the response strategy. Otherwise, if the follow-up is judged to be tone deaf, the problem can be exacerbated rather than ameliorated. We have all seen those public relations nightmares compound as they go viral across social media.

Pacing and Pivoting

How can we adapt to unpredictable changes without collaborating more closely?

You were already dealing with these fast and furious berate, debate, and update loops well before the pandemic, thanks to increased connectivity and prolific social channels that sped up transactions, data cycles, and prevalent public opinion-sharing. However, crisis conditions added new directional dimensions as populations across locales, states, and nations were subject to different restrictions with varying repercussions.

Frequent iterations were necessary for your own business as well as along your supply chain and throughout your ecosystem. Your learned, constant state of preparedness to adapt became characteristic of many executives' mind-frames. Randomly distributed waves of cases and broad-ranging consumer responses generated a cacophony of reactions that could only be met with open, flexible, and empathetic mindsets: *What now? What's new? What's next?* Whatever "had been" was barely relevant in comparison to "what could be" that might keep the business afloat and moving forwards.

You were on it. Like millions of others, to be sufficiently flexible you were ready to explore almost any idea for viability, so real or perceived barriers were dismantled or disappeared. New, urgent cross-corporate cooperation forced people across your organization to rally, connect, and make things happen—to save a revenue stream, a client, their job, the business—and empathy enabled those interactions to be productive.

"Desperate times require desperate measures." So the saying goes. However, many of these measures were long overdue and actually logical developments to facilitate more adaptive general ways of operating. Well-entrenched regimes resisted progress prior to the pandemic's disturbance. Perhaps there was a chat application that some coworkers had wanted to implement or data analytics software that was not deemed necessary because historical analog analysis was assessed to be adequate. Most people had been stuck in old, familiar, and comfortable operating grooves. It did not matter—until crisis struck.

The good news is that the new technology implementations that have now changed digitally enhanced operating practices forever are allowing your company to meet the needs of new business competition. At the same time, it took a global catastrophe to shock us into updating systems and routines that were no longer serving us. Be wary of falling back into old rituals that undermine or replace your new adaptive habits, which allow for changes in business coordination and working circumstances.

During and since the early waves of the pandemic, we practiced critical combinations of interpersonal skills and technical competencies in earnest. We learned to interact seamlessly with colleagues as well as non-employee participants working on a project across multiple locations. These are enduring benefits of our 2020–2021 experiences.

Implementations of chat applications and other instant or asynchronous communications platforms have enabled new communications habits that will keep adapting to the needs of your business. As you rapidly prototype new concepts and offerings, surveying customer sentiment and perspectives, your trials will quickly tell you if you are on the right track and where improvements can be made. Check that your updated operating practices have enough flexibility baked in. Furthermore, regularly check when, rather than if, updates are due.

Working at the current pace of business progress, in individual and close-knit team configurations, and dealing with continued unpredictability about ongoing developments requires us all to be empathetic, open-minded, and receptive to changes to keep up the pace while being ready to pivot. There is no "slow and steady" anymore. No comfortable cruise control. However, we are better managing the volatility after the initial pandemic waves of 2020 and 2021. Rapidly changing and unstable conditions have been swapped for dynamic but (mostly) steady.

Operations disrupted since the pandemic began the need to convert to long-term, stable frameworks and practices adapted for a more digitized era in which conditions have reached a new level of complexity, interconnectivity, and interdependence. This development means repetitive drudgery is often supplanted by more interesting work content. However, an accelerated digital timeframe is resulting in a greater mismatch of skills with less time to reskill and upskill employees.

We also need to lean into our working relationships as we rely more on each other to complete our tasks, adapting as we go in order to collaborate effectively on more complicated, cross-functional, shorter-term projects. Gary A. Bolles, Chair for the Future of Work with Singularity University and author of *The Next Rules of Work*, believes that empathy is one of the key "flex skills" for the future.[3]

Leaning Into Trust

Does our corporate culture foster enough trust among us?

How do you feel when you are with someone you trust? You feel safe. You feel that you could share a more personal story with them, and they would not judge you. You feel you could share a more outlandish idea with them, and they would not criticize or laugh at you. You are in "a psychological state comprising the intention to accept vulnerability and have positive expectations of the intentions or behavior of another."[4]

Trust is not just a psychological state. You also feel more comfortable physically. Your shoulders might relax while you are meeting with this person. Your body may sink deeper into your chair. Your facial expression might soften. Trust is an emotional attitude and often expressed physically.[5]

A lack of trust is experienced in similar ways. You hear a knock at the door late in the evening. It is not someone you know. You do not trust them. You feel afraid and anxious. Your body is tense. Your voice sounds tight as you talk to them. Or, in a work situation, imagine you are meeting with a newly hired executive whom you have only encountered a couple of times. He asks for your frank assessment of certain aspects of your division's operations. What should you say? You do not know this guy yet. You want to be honest and fair. You want to make a good first impression. What would be the appropriate way to mention elements that need attention? You feel stressed. Your throat constricts. Your face feels hot.

When we come together, explore, and appreciate areas of common interest or shared values, we can develop a basic human connection that allows us to form bonds, express ourselves more freely, and take risks. Without the familiarity generated by prior shared knowledge, without any time to empathize and gain confidence about consistent positive interactions—which is the essence of trust—you have not developed mutual understanding with productive commitment as the basis of relationship. Two people are extremely unlikely to feel safe or comfortable enough to speak openly if no trust has been established between them.

Sacha Connor, Founder and CEO of Virtual Work Insider, a consultancy providing hybrid and remote work leadership skills training, recommends kickstarting a new relationship by meeting someone in person if possible.[6] In her eleven years of working remotely, she has found this helps establish the initial trust, which can be hard to achieve through a computer at the beginning of a relationship.

We feel the benefits of developing a sense of belonging. Consider your sense of comfort chatting with several coworkers you trust. These relationships have likely allowed you to share sensitive issues you needed to voice or deliberate on confidentially. Remember too how at the beginning of the pandemic, under much greater strain and pressure, your ability to rely on these connections became critical, especially when needing to solve complicated issues across distributed work settings.

Trust—which enables strong connections between colleagues who can depend on positive outcomes to their interactions—is more essential now that we have moved into Future-of-Work environments. Trusted relationships are critical grounding and enduring facets of our working lives when so much else is in flux. Although the COVID-19 crisis conditions of 2020 and 2021 were extreme and disruptive, general conditions continue to evolve, and we need to assimilate the less volatile, but still dynamic, stability of constant change.

Nurturing enduring, reliable support among colleagues is meaningful as we go through necessary transformations. PwC's Global CEO survey in 2016 reported that 55 percent of CEOs believed a lack of trust was a threat to the growth of their business—this was prior to the pandemic.[7] Trust-based relationships develop when people find others to be mutually dependable, predictable, open, fair, and honest, and act in empathetic and supportive ways. Interactions with a trusted person allow the truster to feel heard, valued, and respected.

People use three predictors to assess others' trustworthiness: ability, benevolence, and integrity. Empathy is a key component of benevolence, which also encompasses other expressions and perceptions of caring, goodwill, responsible fulfillment of obligations, and commitment to goals.[8]

Empathetic bonds between coworkers permit the more open and riskier discussions that are crucial for facilitating the more demanding work interactions we are now tasked with. Consider how, in the past, assignments were generally smaller and simpler and could be accomplished with less interactive debate and cooperation among coworkers and between departments. Think about the multifaceted nature and complexity of the issues and projects your company handled over the last month, especially trying to cater to customers' evolving demands. Creative, adaptive solutions are in great need, taxing teams like never before.

Empathy Drives Innovation

How can we design products and services that match what people really need?

Empathy helps create the safe spaces that encourage everyone to contribute their ideas—however wild—and stimulate the most expansive, productive discussions and brainstorming sessions. All employees—extroverts and introverts—must feel comfortable participating actively, sharing even outlandish ideas, as these may well spark a new thread or idea. To foster the experimentation essential for learning, testing, iterating, and testing again, adopt a design-thinking approach (popularized by design firm IDEO) that is supported by clearly defined "reasonable" risk-taking and forgiveness of failure. We do not herald Thomas Edison as one of the most famous scientific failures of 10,000 experiments. Instead, we focus on the one critical success result and are rarely told how that was derived from his determined, endless iterations. The most effective solutions are generally cultivated through trial and error, especially during transformational times when small modifications to previous configurations can be limited in relevance or applicability, and experimentation of non-incremental adaptations are required.

At the heart of human-centered design's investigation and iterations is empathetic understanding of the target customer in order to develop the most relevant product or service based on potential buyers' actual, versus assumed, needs or desires. Human-centric product design and service development rely heavily on empathy when we are interacting with potential end users to discover what they really mean—not necessarily what they say or think the solution should be. Following extensive, thoughtful questioning to inform a product's or service's development, trials are invaluable to confirm that users' reflections ring true and to refine as needed.

Marketplace turbulence generated by the COVID-19 crisis and perpetuated by Future-of-Work developments meant more frequent reviews and iterations have needed to be scheduled, as customer behaviors adjusted to new circumstances and were pretty fluid at times. In addition, pandemic-related restrictions and other factors that disturbed supply chains impacted the availability of materials and components, leading to lingering effects on business production and output.

Jeremy Fleming, CEO of Stagekings, an Australian event and theater stage construction company, pulled off a stunning pivot in March 2020. Stimulated by empathy for all the employees laid off when all events were canceled, Jeremy thought too about the frustrations of thousands of workers sent home and unable to purchase desks (because of sold-out inventory). In just a few days, Stagekings' skilled craftspeople were fashioning sleek IsoKing desks that were easy to assemble, disassemble, and store. They sold 10,000 in their first three months and kept growing from there.[9] IsoKings is now a permanent multiproduct furniture division of Stagekings.

We need to check, test, edit, confirm, and update the current iterations of our products and services for the anticipated fluctuating needs of potential and existing customers, and how we can best reach and convert them. We need to incorporate flexibility into major strategic decisions to ensure reliable product availability and responsiveness to changing customer requirements—for example, considering where important components are manufactured if we over-rely on supply coming from any particular source.

Emotional Experience

What can we do to support employees dealing with pandemic-related emotional issues?

Empathy is also important to weave into our working lives after the chaos, confusion, and challenges lingering after the emotionality of 2020 and 2021. The intense affront on our psyches caused certain personal/professional boundaries to drop. Brought together in the first wave by a common global crisis, we were connected by our shock and vulnerability. We also were confronted by our own raw emotions and human sensitivities. We were resilient, but we recognized we were not impermeable. We needed each other. It created the conditions for more intimate collaboration and cooperation.

We were assaulted by unexpected volatility and dramatic change, accompanied by extraordinary tragedy and hardship. We had to try to process these shocks while continuing to function sufficiently well—running and supporting our businesses, divisions, teams, and families. We were thrown out of "normal" routines and settings and forced to set up new practices and find new equilibrium—which we had never been tasked with before.

Our individual and combined discomfort, the world over, was evident. It shook us and connected us. Our new work cadence included intermittent periods of vulnerability, and as we saw into each other's homes, we started to understand our common feelings, challenges, and needs. We also began to recognize the greater breadth of others' pain and experiences— some which had started long before.

We started to empathize more. Across and within our work environments. Why? Our natural empathy spilled over into our work lives, as the two were no longer separated artificially by physical distances, office edifices, or conventionally formal and reserved business interactions. On the frontline, we were coping with more intense situations, heightened risks, and unending strain. Polite professional barriers broke down because we needed each other. Empathy became a solution to create elements that could sustain us through the crisis as well as reduce our emotional volatility as we shared the new cadence of stability and vulnerability. Our relationships got stronger and deeper as we reached across geographic divides to support each other, partly in the knowledge of our own future shaky moments.

Now Matthias Hollwich is designing new office buildings in response to these heightened needs—recognizing employees' emotional cadences and experiences—realizing requirements have evolved. Office settings need to bolster the stronger corporate cultures that we are now nurturing to connect and support us across multiple work locations.

Empathetic Aftermath

How do I get my middle managers to treat their teams like human beings?

This is the exact question I was asked in 2018 by a senior Human Resources executive who worked at a company that runs a national network of seniors' living facilities. She was not suggesting that any of these managers were bad people. I do not imagine they treated people poorly in their personal lives. We have siloed our behavior in the past. However, we have been conditioned to the transactional nature of work that employees—from senior executives to fresh associates—have practiced in performing their duties for generations. Within most organizations, the value of work's experiential aspects has only recently been recognized, as well as how corporate values drive behaviors and mindsets. Now, we can imagine how her managers' attitudes towards their teams might have translated into how they treated those under their care during the pandemic.

We have now experienced extreme work conditions—and have been stretched, buffeted, pushed, pulled, shaken, stirred, pummeled, tested, exhausted, suppressed, and also intrigued and enlightened. Think of the range of conditions you have dealt with in your work since March 2020. Reflect upon the highs and lows that you dealt with, that you saw others around you experience, that you reached out to coworkers to talk them through. Remember those burning out during spring 2021 as people were desperate for winter and restrictions to be over. Recall the anxiety that so many employees felt when called back to the office, disturbing their working lives yet again, and then great frustration with new mask mandates and travel restrictions in summer 2021.

We are only able to recognize *and address* the lasting multidimensional psychological impact of the pandemic and the ongoing work-related turmoil that has followed it by practicing empathy. More attentive and empathetic manager oversight is critical so that we can design and transition fully to healthy new routines. Empathetic attention to identify signals helps spot potential issues and acknowledge ongoing heightened sensitivities to crisis triggers and repercussions. Ramped-up mental health and well-being benefits and policies have been absorbing the consequences of the prolonged turbulence and social isolation. However, 48 percent of young employees globally—such as those of Gen Z, who had higher levels of anxiety than other generations prior to 2020[10]— "felt stressed all or most of the time."[11] More Gen Z adults than other generations also reported mental health issues since the pandemic began (for example, 34 percent in the United States; Generation X was the next highest at 21 percent).[12] Gen Zs benefit from attentive, active support to reset their outlook and turn around recent work experiences, but they often do not feel comfortable speaking up.

We have also benefited. We have gained important, fundamental learnings from what we have gone through. With no forewarning, we had to figure out and adapt, and we managed to achieve so much more than we ever thought possible under emergency situations. We always had the capabilities, but not the impetus or urgent need to execute. Think back to recent times when you astonished yourself with what you were actually able to achieve. Under more stable conditions, when not rallying to overcome extraordinary disruption, what if you could accomplish much more, without significant effort, just by tapping into your innate abilities? What if you could understand and apply more of what you already know— especially about interacting productively with colleagues— and could better focus everyone's energy, including your own?

When we integrate empathy into our corporate culture and professional interactions and have a choice of environments we can match with our daily cadence—of the type that

Matthias Hollwich is creating—we *will* naturally be treating each other like human beings. We will then also foster the best chance of achieving our "flow"; encouraging productive discussions; inspiring, trialing, and executing our best ideas; and generating sustainable competitive advantage.

Empathy Takeaways

- Empathy is integral as a core cultural value, mindset, and critical skill for the new era of work, where the emphasis is on people's experiences.

- Narrow targeting of products and services means understanding more about the individuals who compose your audience and using empathetic messaging.

- Practicing empathy allows people to work together more effectively and respond under faster-paced, more stressful, and uncertain conditions.

- Trust is essential to build strong relationships, foster a sense of belonging, and create safe spaces where people feel comfortable to speak up, share ideas, and innovate.

- The pandemic crisis elevated the need for empathetic mutual understanding and support.

3

How Empathy Works

REMEMBER THE last video conference you joined when a colleague was frustrated, whether they were unable to get the audio at the office connected properly, or they were calling in from the street and the connection kept dropping, or their flight got canceled because of weather and they could not get to a good WiFi location because of traffic? You felt their stress, their urgent energy as they strived to resolve the problem. You have been there so many times. *Argh!*

You connected with their emotions and may have felt your heart rate rise and muscles stiffen, both because the situation awakened similar memories and feelings in you and because you also knew the person well, knew what they were thinking and how they looked and sounded when stressed out. You tuned in to their tension, even from miles away. This is empathy at work: as a series of sparked connections between two people, as the brain neurons of one mirror and actively simulate the situation affecting the other.

Dutch primatologist Frans de Waal calls empathy "a human universal" and "part of our evolution, and not just a recent part, but an innate, age-old capacity. Relying on automated sensitivities to faces, bodies, and voices, humans empathize from day one."[1] However, the word only showed up in English in 1909. It was a translation of the German word "*Einfühlung*"—literally "in-feeling"—to describe how we connect or "feel into" works of art or nature.[2] The word itself was devised by German philosopher Rudolf Lotze, from the Greek "*empatheia*," the word for passion that combines "en-," meaning "in," and "pathos," which means "feeling."[3]

Practically, how does each person involved register this "in-feeling" of empathy? Recognition of mutual understanding and emotions stimulates a deeper connection. One person uses empathy to bridge the physical separation between them and "feeling into" what the other person is going through. The sensation, however much or little it is perceived, affords the person empathizing a fuller understanding of the other's perspective and experience. The person empathized with, in turn, receives the sensation of being heard, seen, and understood, which is generally interpreted positively as feeling valued and respected.

Empathy is considered one of the "soft" skills. I find this counterintuitive, as many people find it harder to practice empathy skills in professional exchanges than applying "hard," functional skills. Psychological and emotional connection and engagement require attention and great effort for many people, especially in work settings where elevated use of interpersonal skills has not previously been common.

Indeed, far from being "soft," empathy puts you in a *stronger* position as you become more aware of the other person *and* the entire scenario, rather than just your own perspective. With insights derived from empathetic understanding about another's view of the situation, as well as tapping into their actual emotional state, you can have a more relevant discussion or make a more informed decision. But how *do* you connect in this multidimensional way with another person? Let's get a little nerdy on a human scale, to better transact and interact in our global, multicultural business environment.

Empathy is the term given to a neurological reaction when our brains respond to an external event that happens to someone or possibly something. Typically, specific neurons are stimulated by our own experiences through our nerves or other sensations. However, in the case of empathy, particular neurons in our brains react to what we understand to be another person's experience taking in external inputs. Your brain's reflecting response—by aptly named "mirror neurons"—creates the illusion of a shared sensation, reflecting what we see or hear.

In her book *The Empathy Effect*, Dr. Helen Riess of Harvard Medical School explains how the experience is less acute than if the same situation happened to us, which means we can still act in a way that is supportive, restorative, or preventative for the future.[4] From an anthropological perspective, if we experience some degree of the same joy or pain, we will move further towards or away from the possibility of similar situations in future, boosting or protecting us. Moreover, demonstrating such behavior, we are subconsciously trying to influence others to act the same way towards us in case we are the ones with something to celebrate or wanting comfort next time. Therefore, empathy is at the core of *all* human relationships and lays the foundation for collaboration, cooperation, and reciprocity.

The "Trust Hormone"

Scientists continue to discover more each year about how empathy works. The hormone oxytocin is involved in empathetic interactions. This is a naturally occurring neurochemical—in fact, a "neuropeptide"—that most mammals produce.

Multiple research projects have discovered how oxytocin is involved in a variety of physiological and psychological processes that span blood pressure, birthing, sexual arousal, and social behaviors.

Oxytocin is understood to facilitate the development of social connections and relationships and boost positive communications and assumed social support. This important hormone also reduces negative emotional responses and the impact of anxiety and stressors in social situations.[5] Oxytocin increases a person's empathy, as well as reduces their fear of trusting someone they do not know.

Further research investigated if oxytocin might also play a role in how well someone can read another person's state of mind. Being able to gauge others' mental and emotional states is key to how we all engage socially and assess how trustworthy someone is. The tests were originally developed to assess disorders relating to autism and measure disruptions of social mentalization functions. Newly framed, the tests are some of the most specific ones devised to evaluate components of empathy and how well people can connect with others' internal states. Those given oxytocin in the experiment were noticeably better at distinguishing what people were thinking and feeling in a series of photos that showed only the area around a person's eyes.[6] The study participants more accurately chose words that captured their sentiments from a selection.

Paul J. Zak's research on trust has revealed that the act of a leader reaching out for help—rather than just issuing commands—generates oxytocin in team members, increasing the team's trust in the leader.[7] This outreach prompts people to cooperate naturally. Using this data, if you solicit more inputs as a leader, you can stimulate better relationships and teamwork. In contrast, high-stress situations or stress-generating activities inhibit oxytocin. Consequently, we are functionally less able to trust and empathize with each other during a crisis—just when we need to be able to work together to survive and emerge from the difficult situation. However, if your team has already established trust before an emergency arises, you will be better able to handle it.

Three Steps

Fascinating stuff, right? But what does that all mean for you and understanding empathy's components? How can we improve our natural empathy skills? What are the practical steps involved? How does empathy work as an integral, guiding value to influence people's behaviors? How can you exercise your own skills and apply empathy in work situations to your benefit?

To understand empathy infused in action, there are three key components: Cognitive Empathy, Affective Empathy, and Empathetic Action. I translate these practically into three steps—THINK, FEEL, and ACT—which communicate how to incorporate (more) empathy into your daily habits when interacting with anyone, from customers to colleagues to contractors.

- THINK: Cognitive Empathy relates to perspective-taking, recognizing that another person has their own way of seeing and thinking about the world. It does not mean you necessarily agree with the person's point of view, but you actively seek to see things through their eyes, using your imagination and curiosity. A basic example in a work setting is how you and others decide to celebrate someone's birthday: What kind of cake would they like? Which pub or restaurant would they prefer to go to after work? Would they like a surprise celebration with balloons, or would something low-key be best? You have put yourself in their shoes to think about their preferences, rather than create the kind of celebration that you would enjoy.

- FEEL: Affective Empathy is the shared emotional response in which we can sense what the other person is going through—we feel it *with* them. There are two parts: (1) identifying the specific emotion the person is feeling, and hopefully confirming you are correct; and (2) connecting with their experience. Using the birthday example, you might have gone so far as to think of your colleague's face turning white and feeling them recoil if they were caught unawares. Or you may have projected how uncomfortable they would feel if you all went to the lively bar *you* like—no, that place would not be right; it is *their* birthday, after all!

- ACT: Deriving from your comprehension of another person's perspective and their sentiment about a situation, Empathetic Action is what you choose to do as a consequence, generally driven by compassion, desiring a positive outcome. One such example would be where you helped organize the birthday celebration for your coworker and purchased the kind of cake they like or booked a table at the quaint café they often go to. You might decide not to act differently based on your new knowledge; moreover, Empathetic Action *can* also be negative. Manipulative people can use their empathy skills to get what they want. Highly empathetic people, often known as "empaths," may be easily bulldozed into doing what another person wants. They need determination to delineate explicit boundaries to protect themselves. We do generally assume and expect people to use their attuned understanding for significant overall benefit. But ethical practice of empathy is important to communicate and demonstrate, so that you and those you influence put your empathy-gleaned understanding to good use.

These empathy components are not definitive but match what Stephanie Preston and Frans de Waal report in their theory connecting interpersonal perception and action monitoring how the brain works when someone tunes in to another person emotionally.[8] Other descriptions or categorizations exist; however, the essence of the definitions is similar. Daniel Goleman uses the term "Emotional Empathy,"[9] building upon his seminal work on emotional intelligence, of which empathy is one of the five components.[10] Michael Ventura, author of *Applied Empathy*, uses "Somatic Empathy."[11] Both these terms are closely equivalent to Affective Empathy, aiming to capture the physical sensation that is part of empathizing—created by emotional states. For instance, if someone feels very embarrassed, *your* face might also get hot and flush red; if another is really scared, *you* might get goose bumps too. Empathetic Action is also described as "Empathic Concern" by Goleman.[12] Both refer to the effective consequences that empathizing is anticipated to result in. Everyone's work in this field is building up our understanding and bringing new data, intelligence, and specificity.

Cognitive Empathy

This element of empathy is perhaps the hardest to get your head around—almost literally! It is also the core, and probably the most useful, part of practicing empathy skills in work situations. Perspective-taking, recognizing that no one else sees the world quite the way you do, helps you appreciate where someone is coming from and the reasons behind their actions.

The intention is to find a way to move mentally around to the other person's side of the table and see an issue as they do. When you can manage that, you will find some common ground that allows you to bridge your differences in a negotiation or develop a solution amidst conflict. In his work, Michael Ventura focuses heavily on this aspect of empathy, which is a critical practice in his core brand strategy business.[13] Everyone involved in developing and executing effective campaigns and initiatives must understand how their clients' customers think and what they want.

How can you understand an issue from an angle other than your own? What are the best ways to think about a topic or matter with new eyes? It starts with *deliberately* expanding your mental range of vision—pushing out the boundaries of what you explore and feel comfortable with.

EXERCISE 1: Consider a colleague who has a very different opinion than you about a work-related topic. Activate your curiosity about *why* they have that point of view. Do they not know what you know? What have they missed? There is also the nagging question: Is there something that you might have missed or not paid sufficient attention to? Stimulating your imagination, asking yourself more questions, helps you to engage and explore their perspective, and yours, to see where they overlap.

At the same time, emphasize where your opinions already converge or are aligned. When you identify common ground and can cultivate some sense of connection, you will feel closer to them mentally. The task becomes easier—there is no longer a chasm you have to leap to understand them. Later on, isolate the specifics of select differences. Do they now seem more resolvable? With better comprehension of these details, you can create a more complete picture of how the person understands the situation, as well as generate possible solutions.

I am a dog person—I have two. I do not *dislike* cats, but I am not a cat person. Why? I find cats—and admittedly there are exceptions—can act haughty, dismissive, and standoffish. In comparison, generally, dogs are affectionate, are dependent, and seem mostly content. My interactions with many cats have left me feeling slighted, tolerated, and even used!

However, I decided to empathize with a dear friend I was visiting who has cats. I withheld my normal reaction and reframed my point of view to experience hers. I love animals, as my friend does, which was our common ground and my starting point. I therefore observed and appreciated her cats' more distant presence and companionship, as well as their feline elegance. I also recognized the benefits of not being followed around everywhere and not being bothered for attention when busy. There was still a mutually rewarding relationship, but it was just weighted and timed differently. I am still a dog person—I love their floppy friendliness and enthusiasm, and I love to take long hikes with them in the forest or along the beach. But I am now open to the idea of having a cat too someday!

Affective Empathy

Why is connecting emotionally important? If you understand how someone thinks about a situation, it does not necessarily mean you understand how they feel about it. It is all too easy to overlay how *you* would react in the circumstances, drawing on your own background, context, knowledge, and potential to be set off by your particular triggers. Realizing where your own sensitivities and landmines are is one thing; discerning where or what each of your colleagues' or team members' are is quite another.

The first part of Affective Empathy is distinguishing the emotion that the other person is feeling, so that you can connect with their authentic state. Some people's faces are easy to read—they really do "wear their emotions on their sleeve," as the saying goes! However, other people's faces are more cryptic, and their emotions can be much harder to figure out, which requires that you pay attention to additional signals and clues to assess their feelings correctly. You decode someone's signals like a detective without realizing it.

"Yes, I've been practicing reading my emotions and I'm getting the hang of it!"

EXERCISE 2: This week, pay keen attention when a couple of your reports interact with you—in person and online—to assess their mindset, mood, and energy level, by noticing their

- VOICE: Are they talking fast? Do they sound breathy or tense? Is their pitch high?

- LANGUAGE: Do they sound hesitant, making unusual grammatical mistakes? Are they speaking or writing more casually than normal? Did they lag in their answers or hardly respond?

- BODY LANGUAGE: Are they leaning in with interest or away? How casual is their posture? Are they moving their hands more than usual? Are they sitting calmly or shifting in their chair?

- MEDIUM: Did they use their preferred or a different channel? Was their communication briefer or more lengthy than usual, and did the channel suit the content?

- DEMEANOR: What is their bearing and behavior like relative to previous interactions? When you are familiar with someone's typical deportment, you have a consistent baseline for comparison.

How did that go? Was it easy or hard to work out what they were feeling? You already decode these cues naturally with your family, your friends, and the colleagues you know well. With coworkers you are not as familiar with, were you able to work out their emotion from the way they were talking or sitting? What was the key indicator? Were you sensitized to slight changes in cadence or tone when they responded? Was it something you observed in their facial expression or body language? Or did you notice different timing of their written communication? Nice detective work! Whatever cues you picked up, you will notice more from now on. Remember, when all signals are consistent with the emotion you believe they are feeling, it is always a good idea to check, to be sure your assessment of their mood is accurate.

Then it is time to tap into their experience. Why? Sharing an emotional state with someone gives you the best connection with their perspective and helps separate you from *your* opinion, reaction, or attitude. With more sense of what they are going through, you naturally understand their reasoning better. At the very least, they feel heard and understood, which enhances the chance of positive outcomes.

EXERCISE 3: As you identify your colleagues' emotion, lean into your existing mental connection to enhance it with feeling—whether they are experiencing joy or anger or frustration or sadness or disappointment. Recognize your own initial reaction to the situation so you can more easily put it aside and proactively engage in *their* state of mind. Then, just as you have been emotionally carried away watching a movie or live sports game or listening to a friend's drama, recognize when you tune in to their feeling, sensing it rising within you, and ride it fully. It certainly may not be how *you* would feel. You are mirroring and being carried by the other person's feelings. When you consciously connect more deeply with their experience, you are deliberately empathizing with them and developing greater capacity and skills. This exercise is harder than the others in this chapter, so it may take a while to get the hang of it. You've got this!

Is it possible to empathize without truly feeling as the other person does? Yes, although you have less understanding about their experience. As many people do, you may find it hard or even stressful to deal with other people's emotions. If so, being curious about someone's point of view and recognizing how they feel still greatly increases your ability to act empathetically, as well as ensures the other person feels heard and valued.

Empathetic Action

What matters now is how you act based on all the understanding you have gained. If you generally have a good idea about how to proceed before talking to others, your vision and direction are valuable—as contributions to the solution. However, putting those thoughts to one side is helpful. You might write them down to shape and clarify them yourself, while also keeping them open as tentative, rather than definitive. Even strong opinions can be held lightly and make for good, rigorous debate! You would also naturally resist changing any pre-decided course of action. In an evolving business climate, you can solve complex issues more easily by exploring and incorporating a range of diverse perspectives. Moreover, those involved are more committed to the solution with a sense of ownership.

EXERCISE 4: Identify a small matter needing a decision, and bring relevant parties together early in the process. Hear all perspectives fully, listening actively and asking thoughtful questions. Especially if you are the most senior person involved, facilitating the discussion—and not actively participating—is your most beneficial role, putting your opinion, and any contemplated pre-determined conclusion, aside. With all gathered inputs, help integrate the information shared to build the case for the optimal outcome. Afterwards, contrast the result with your initial position and observe where new data benefited the final result.

As we deal with greater complexity, it behooves us to have inclusive mindsets, assess multiple points of view, and solicit and incorporate relevant data before we make a decision. Empathetic discussion invites participants to contribute and build on one another's ideas, allows people to challenge each other respectfully, and results in a thoughtfully and thoroughly discussed conclusion.

Empathetic Optimization

Another important aspect of the brain science relates to the parts of your brain that are activated over the course of your workday. Of course, we all want the most developed and sophisticated areas engaged—for ourselves and our teams. In fact, we *need* these areas functioning properly so that each person can apply themselves fully to the opportunities and problems at hand.

However, consider what happened the last time you started your workday in a bad mood. Your temper was set off by a terrible commute, an irate boss, or a coworker's hapless mistake. The rest of your day might have been off kilter; perhaps a cascading series of incidents followed, including bad interactions and suboptimal decisions you made.

Why does this happen? These types of negative incidents trigger your brain into heightened emotional states. Your brain capacity is more constrained, focused on "danger" mode. Your cognitive range and mental capacity are physiologically constrained, potentially leading to more simplistic and emotionally driven decision-making when contemplating a complicated issue. Can you recall a recent situation when a coworker responded uncharacteristically poorly after a prior situation or comment had destabilized them? Caroline Webb, author and Founder of How to Have a Good Day, an advisory firm focused on the science of high performance in the workplace, explains, "There is less activity in the prefrontal cortex when people feel even mildly stressed by something they can't control. It's normal not to be at our best under uncomfortable pressure."[14]

Reduced mental capacities caused by varying levels of crisis mode since the start of the pandemic have severely affected people's ability to work effectively. You saw that in team members' periods of burnout, as well as in days or weeks when you knew you were not delivering your best work. Under more stable conditions, while in this mental and emotional state temporarily, it is hard for any person to contribute fruitfully in a meeting or to a discussion. Not only could their inputs be disruptively off-point or simplistic and their contributions lower-quality, but also less thoughtful responses or tones could potentially trigger counterproductive reactions in other team members. Empathy works by enabling you to tap into others' emotional experiences—including recognizing when anyone is in an overly elevated state—so you can act quickly to mitigate the situation.

Empathy also sensitizes you to when others have noticed a heightened emotional state that might have been triggered in *you*. You might not have paid enough attention before to irritation set off, for example, by a repetitive, negative family dynamic that a colleague mimics. Have you ever noticed coworkers registering surprise as they interact with you or casting sideways glances at each other? In a charged emotional condition, you are unlikely to be able to connect with anyone else's emotion. However, if you notice certain facial expressions and reactions, you can check your own pulse rate or flushed sensation to see if you feel out of sorts or less at ease than normal.

Managing the Emotion

You can cope with your peaks and those of others. When you feel it in your chest or your face, or sense someone else's elevated emotional state, by reacting quickly you can make a significant difference. As Caroline puts it, "You need a repertoire for noticing, pausing, and then resetting."[15] Intense attention or limited diverting action can pull the plug on any further drama, so the situation does not escalate. The objective is to diminish your sense of danger so that your brain shifts out of its emotional operating mode.

You can use several methods. Two, in particular, may be the easiest to apply in work settings:

- BREATHING: Concentration on calm, measured breathing stimulates the production of gamma-aminobutyric acid (GABA), which reduces nerve and neural activity. Box breathing is a helpful technique that involves three steps, counting to four slowly at each step: (1) breathing in; (2) holding your breath; and (3) exhaling through your mouth.[16] Repeating these steps, you soon feel much calmer, are able to physiologically restabilize yourself, and re-engage the higher-functioning part of your brain. If you can pause from contributing actively in a meeting for just one minute, you may be able to turn things around quietly while still seated.

- DIVERSION: In many work situations, the most effective approach is often to create a productive distraction—especially if you are trying to manage someone else's triggered state. You can suggest a "bio" break during a meeting, generating five minutes for people to get up, stretch their legs, and reset. Or, if you or other attendees need time to recalibrate before a meeting starts, a minor postponement for catching up with others or a technical check can provide the time and space needed.

Other helpful techniques for managing emotions include "labeling" and "reframing," which are more involved but worth investigating if you find stress and anxiety regularly degrade your interactions and hinder your productivity.

The critical aspect here, in my opinion, is that empathetic acknowledgment of each other's triggers and understanding that certain things can set any one of us off allows us to give ourselves and each other a break. We have lived through times when we revealed great vulnerability to each other. Learning from that experience, we can take thoughtful steps, then re-engage and not try and push through suboptimally when our ability to think clearly and work effectively is greatly inhibited. We can be on guard to mitigate situations where anyone has reduced capacity, as current conditions require everyone's fullest possible participation, especially when we have learned positive, proactive measures we can take to turn things around.

Blocking Behaviors

In 2018, my mother called me after the side of her car had been smashed into overnight while parked in the rather narrow street she lived on in Oxford, England. She was upset about the damage to the vehicle, but we soon determined that it was more superficial than serious. We discussed the repairs, which, together with my sister, I offered to cover.

That was the end of it as far as I was concerned, but my mother returned to the subject at least three more times during the conversation. She was pretty distraught. I didn't get it. On the one hand, I was certainly outraged and frustrated that someone could hit her car and take off. On the other hand, the car was still drivable and she didn't have to pay for the repairs. However, I could feel and hear how distressed she was.

It wasn't until we had hung up and I reflected on *her* point of view that I started to understand. That car represented her freedom, her ability to go her painting classes and her yoga lessons and to see her friends. Her car connected her with her community and was critical for her emotional sustenance. While she had sounded relieved when she confirmed that the car was still roadworthy, she was probably anxious to think of the days she would be without it while it was being repaired.

I had not been empathetic at all. I had looked at the incident from my perspective, with my logic, and had only accounted for how I would react if the same thing had happened to me. But, it wasn't me; it was my mother, whose age, reduced physical mobility, and location in Oxford put more importance on her need for a car. When I tapped into her mood, I could feel her anxiety about being disconnected from her friends and her stress about being isolated when it went to be repaired.

Judgments block our ability to empathize if we focus on our own point of view and reaction and jump to ill-formed conclusions. Did you ever receive an email that annoyed you, and you responded in irritation, only to find out that you had misinterpreted the person's note? Your mistake ended up causing upset on the other side, and you created an unnecessary hole you had to dig yourself out of, which took a while!

We all have opinions and make judgments. Some people are more vocal about their opinions and make quicker assessments than others, but we all have them. Judgments are natural and can be very helpful in evaluating a situation or person, particularly in challenging circumstances when a quick reaction may be important to keep us out of harm's way. In less dramatic conditions, opinions based on insufficient data or erroneous assumptions can also influence our subsequent actions.

What if you put aside your own perspective and initial response and focus on the other person? When you step away from your own opinion and any simmering judgment, you can better understand *their* experience and state of mind. You are better equipped to recognize their meaning, and if you are not sure, you can email back first for more information before you send out a stinging reply that ends up hurting you.

Now you have the steps to practicing empathy. However, to integrate it into your work life, there is a bit more you need to know.

Empathy Takeaways

- Empathy has three steps:

  Think: Consider the other person's perspective—how they see and think about the world.

  Feel: Discover, and confirm, then tap into what the other person is going through.

  Act: Proceed based on the additional information gathered from the first two steps.

- Using calm, deep breathing or a short distraction are effective options to manage your own and others' elevated emotional states.

- Judgments block the ability to empathize, so step away from your reaction and focus on the other person's.

4

Empathy Starts with You

M Y PERSONAL journey with empathy started within a family of forceful personalities. It took me years to recognize how childhood experiences are affected by the empathy experienced between family members. How much their needs and desires were fulfilled, or not, greatly affects how people evolve as maturing children rising into adulthood, as Steven Kessler explains in *The 5 Personality Patterns*—however hard our parents tried, or we try if parents ourselves![1] We can be unaware of patterns of behavior derived from imbalances we learned as children and that, over time, determine how much we focus on our own needs or default to emphasizing the needs of others.

We have all noticed cases of extreme imbalances; for instance, where one person is railroaded or overwhelmed by others' requests of them, which I have seen a few deeply empathetic people experience. Other visible extremes happen when narcissistic individuals do not consider other people's perspectives or feelings and are only focused on themselves.

Whatever the initial cause or source of these behavioral patterns, for healthy relationships with healthy exchanges—in our personal and professional lives—the objective is to achieve a relative balance, where both or all parties' needs are sufficiently addressed. Do you have a sense of your needs in a conversation with family or friends? How about at work?

Working in the Dark

Self-awareness has not been a priority in traditional work-places, based on the very constrained conditions we have been working under. We were given few choices. Standardized and regimented, industrialized work settings did not encourage individualization or reward individuality, so most of us dedicated little time to employment-related self-reflection about alternatives, unless it was specifically career-related.

Instead, we tried to be as productive as possible based on the parameters of the role we were in, fit the mold, and performed as best we could. Or we changed jobs, which was not generally well received, nor was changing disciplines or sectors appreciated if we had not lucked upon a field our skills or interests happened to be aligned well with. Work has been *expected* to be a relatively unpleasant part of our lives, which we were compensated for but that unpleasantness was, in part, deliberate. Indeed, Protestant ethic, especially in the Calvinist view, attached value to hard work as one sign of someone's eternal salvation.[2]

Gallup has plotted the sorry story of our overall lack of engagement in our work for years, reporting in their 2021 "State of the Global Workplace" that only 20 percent of the global population was engaged in 2020, down from a long-term "high" of 22 percent globally in 2019.[3] Mental discon-nection from our jobs also resulted from the lack of autonomy or alignment with our passions, never mind the omission of logical orientation of our work towards our strengths or skills. It is no wonder that prior to the pandemic the global economy had experienced a decade of broad-based decline in productivity growth after reaching a peak of 2.7 percent in 2007.[4] We had no incentive or inclination or reason to imagine what we could do instead. So we didn't.

The good news is that we have moved on from this legacy of doctrine-influenced negative work attitudes. We thankfully are no longer bound by the physical constraints that kept us in close proximity to all the machines. We have upgraded from the unsophisticated technology that caused the drives for mass standardization to achieve economies of scale.

We are now identifying, focusing on, understanding, *and serving* the individual—as potential buyers or hires, as clients, colleagues, and ourselves. It is time to acknowledge fully the current realities of our time and our work. This is the moment to step up, lean in, and find out what we want from our lives—for ourselves and others around us—so we can create the world and environments that we want to engage in.

Who Am I?

"Who am I?" is undeniably a big question, and developing your answer is an important part of becoming more self-aware. We each have many layers to peel back and there are numerous ways to achieve greater self-knowledge. We all have our different approaches and comfort with personal exploration for a myriad of reasons. I would not begin to prescribe any particular methodology or any destination for anyone else, particularly as this is the texture of life's rich tapestry that you weave for yourself.

But attaining some clarity about what matters to you in your life and how work helps you achieve—or gets in the way of—that is important. I believe that it also enhances the possibility of you accomplishing your goals if you proactively smooth certain wrinkles in the fabric of your life and identify areas where you get triggered. When do you occasionally react disproportionately, where subconscious patterns of behavior might be derailing you in particular situations or with particular individuals you work with?

This is where empathy has always been useful to mitigate the negative effects of our different personal histories as we convene in pairs and groups to complete tasks. Empathy helps us foster more mutually equitable interactions and have fruitful conversations. With heightened self-awareness, we can defuse some of our own issues first, reducing the barriers to productive discussion. We can uncover and eliminate triggers that others might set off unknowingly, and better understand others' triggers, giving us more appreciation of our coworkers and greater ability to contribute to positive discourse.

What Do You Want?

It has been an eye-opening journey since 2011, when I first forayed into the early stages of the field that became the "Future of Work." I set up my own company, Flexcel Network, which focused on workplace flexibility from the outset. I started finding out about people's attitudes, commitments, and reactions to work. Between 2011 and 2020, I asked hundreds and hundreds of people:

> *If you could design your perfect job, what would it look like?*

The response from over 95 percent of people was a momentary flash of excitement—about the idea, the possibilities, the freedom—followed quickly by a blank expression as they realized they had no clue. Since they had never felt they had a choice, they had not embarked on what would have been a fruitless project, an exercise in frustration. Why ever consider what they would *really* like to do, when and where they would like to do it, and how, if they would never be able to realize it? Have you ever explored what your "perfect job" would be?

Interestingly, similar reactions were as true of employees working eighty- to one-hundred-hour weeks wanting more "work/life balance" as those looking to get back into the corporate workforce after some years providing childcare in the home. In fact, those seeking to return to company employment were at least sensitized to certain demands they were no longer prepared to fulfill. It appeared their time away from corporate environments had given many a more balanced sense of what mattered across all their life's activities.

The discussions that flowed from people's answers amassed data that verified the common themes from my own months-long, multistage journey exploring my perfect job. I had wanted to set myself up with more flexible work conditions to juggle my work and family life better, with two kids. Notably, back in 2010, finding something I enjoyed was a low-level consideration rather than being a top priority. However, how could I choose what to do if I had no idea what I needed? How could I develop and adopt self-affirming and mutually beneficial patterns of behavior to be able to nurture a successful, sustainable, and healthy professional career? Continuing unhealthy patterns of behavior when we interact with others at work undermines our ability to achieve our goals.

As I tried to define my new what, where, and how of work, I found I was not clear about what I wanted. I started due diligence on my working life, very practically focused on workplace flexibility, which was an identifiable specific need— to better accommodate my children and my work. I learned much about myself in the progress, including other needs.

Many people start their journey because of one particular pain point they are obliged to adapt for, which then opens the possibility of substantial consideration of "What *do* I want?"

Epiphany Episodes

We are facing a bigger picture here—enabled by technology and catalyzed by COVID-19-related conditions and trauma. New possibilities and necessities about reconfiguring the parameters of our working lives started people "epiphany-quitting" their jobs in the summer of 2021. That August, Frances McLeod, Owner and Founding Partner of Forensic Risk Alliance, a multinational regulatory compliance, disputes, and investigations consultancy, noted a couple of surprising departures—one being a forensic accounting partner returning to school to become a nurse and do something "more meaningful."[5]

So many began rethinking the whole of their lives. We have an unprecedented period to engage in redefining our lives in general: what we are doing, how and where; what choices we are making for the short- and medium-term; what directions we are considering for the future and why. What are your ambitions for your life—personally and professionally? This is where we are now. This moment affords us proactive intention of discovery and design. How involved are you in actively crafting your life, as well as influencing the shape of things to come?

Locked down at home or in risky frontline roles, with new restricted perspectives of our world combined with the challenges of crisis conditions, we were almost forced to reflect on the configurations of our lives and work. Alternate arrangements suddenly seemed viable and possible to consider.

We are now going through a critical inflection period when so much is in flux, when so much more is possible, enabled, and empowered. Our world is going through a particularly dynamic transformational phase, and your intentional participation is, I believe, crucial for your personal and professional satisfaction and success, as well as that of your business.

Having an epiphany that things can be different, even "should" be different, is the first tiny step. All the work follows. Recognizing your own responses as you deliberate about your life enhances your ability to relate to, empathize with, and support your coworkers' and team members' multi-month process to figure out what they want, often crystallizing many elements for the first time. You and your organization can also then be prepared, be present, and even participate in employees' "epiphany" journeys, helping them explore other arrangements or internal opportunities.

You may have discovered a satisfying configuration for your working life a while ago. If so, congratulations! Or it's a work in progress, as for most people who are some way through contemplating new combinations for their entire—integrated and more balanced—life, making plans, and taking action. Instead of waiting for inevitable fallout, with resignations as more people re-evaluate their situations, your company can support and accommodate changes.

EXERCISE: Benefit from a better understanding of yourself at work and increase your comprehension of how others can improve their situations and results by developing and recording a clear picture of the overall best work schedule and configuration for yourself. Your "optimal working profile" is my term for your naturally occurring work-related preferences. Learning (more) about yourself and paying attention to details and differences allows you to refine and optimize your work timing and settings so you know how to maximize your "flow" state and performance.

As you overtly discern the most important factors to you, you can more easily recognize and adapt for others' optimal priority working modes and manner. You are also better equipped to maximize team performance and encourage empathizing among team members to compromise over each other's lower-priority factors. Below are some questions to consider. You likely know some, but not all, of the answers already, with personal interests and obligations necessarily interwoven with professional ones as work/life boundaries are increasingly blurred.

To discover your work-related priorities, which incorporate future desires and career growth, it is important to reflect upon many aspects of your work and overall life experiences. Your answers to key foundational questions form the framework and boundaries of any new configuration of your working life. As you progress through the list below, observe yourself, ask people for input, and remember their comments. Collated, this data provides you with broad-based understanding to inform your reflection and decisions.

For a more detailed list of questions and worksheet, please go to empathyworks.online to further explore and develop your optimal working profile, just as you can help others do.

Consider these questions:

FUNDAMENTALS

- FULFILLMENT: What satisfaction are you getting from your work content, role, and community? What ambitions do you have for your career—achieving, learning, contributing, and more?

- FINANCIAL SECURITY: Are you being suitably compensated yet, with reasonable stability? What type of employment arrangement do you prefer?

- HEALTH: Are you comfortable with your overall and specific well-being support? What causes you the most anxiety and stress, and what can you adjust to manage them effectively? Does your work support a healthy lifestyle/fitness routine?

- HAPPINESS: Do you feel a sense of belonging at work? Is your individual development and success being nurtured? Does your work environment support your emotional well-being? Does your overall living environment support your well-being?

- CONTENT: What kind of work do you enjoy doing, that satisfies you intellectually, emotionally, spiritually, or physically? Which tasks do you complete easily, and which do you struggle with? What kind of projects do you engage in most?

- DEAL BREAKERS: What non-negotiable specifications impact your working life? They may be location-based, cost-related, lifestyle-dependent, family-based, or values-driven.

FEATURES

- OVERSIGHT: What kind of management support maximizes your output—high touch with many check-ins, a hands-off approach, or some other combination?

- SKILLS: What are your top three skills? How are you developing and sustaining your professional competitive advantage?

- CAREER: What role or career are you considering next and why? What do you need to take the next step?

FUNCTION

- TIMING: When do you feel most energized and awake and easily able to focus? When do you need to take a time-out as your energy levels fall?

- LOCATION: Where are you most focused—at home, the office, or a third location? What type of space supports or distracts you?

- SITUATION: Do you prefer to work as part of a team or alone? Does it energize or distract you to be surrounded by the buzz of people around you? What else supports your concentration?

- OBLIGATIONS: What unavoidable overlap of responsibilities from your personal life (such as childcare, elder care, and community commitments) must be considered in devising your optimal working profile?

These questions take time and thought to respond to. Your answers will inform a journey of intentional discovery as you identify and gather pieces of information to help you visualize a more complete picture of yourself and your future. This exercise is a multistage, multi-month process to investigate all that you want for a fulfilling working life, encompassing the psychological and emotional aspects as well as the operating mechanics and logistics. If you have not explored all these elements of your life yet, the process is revealing and worthwhile.

Wherever you are in the process, reflections since the start of the pandemic can help inform and guide you as you amass all necessary inputs. We learned a lot more about ourselves during the extremely restrictive, crisis-related conditions: about our preferred work habits, how isolation affects us, and how regular connection with coworkers supports our well-being. We started to appreciate our own vulnerabilities and when we needed to take a break or pay attention to rising stress or anxiety. We also realized more about what matters and what does not.

Of course, your optimal working profile picture needs to be a dynamic document rather than a snapshot. We evolve in increments and jumps, and our situations do too—when milestone events occur. We age, and our life stage, careers, and skills advance. Different personal circumstances also progress—kids grow up and parents grow old.

For those seeking to perform at high levels in conditions that are more dynamic and unpredictable than we were used to pre-2020, greater self-awareness—about what you want from life and what matters to you—yields important benefits. A core advantage is your improved understanding of who you are working with and what motivates, drives, and distracts them. You can use new intelligence and learnings about yourself to connect with and develop more productive relationships with your coworkers and reports.

Empathy Takeaways

- Achieving greater self-awareness enhances your ability to empathize more easily and connect with others' points of view and experiences.

- Define and refine your optimal working profile to be deliberate about how you configure your working life and recognize colleagues' professional needs and considerations.

- Proactive support of employees' journeys of discovery helps your company recognize and respond—as desired—to their concerns and changes.

- We have the opportunity to modify the framework of our lives significantly—where are you (and your coworkers) in that process?

5

But It's about Them

"**W**HAT ON EARTH?!"
Can you recall a time recently when a potential customer suddenly disengaged or a colleague did something that completely surprised you? You were really taken aback by how they acted, perhaps frustrated by the possible derailment of a plan or project phase. "What happened? Why did they do that?" You were expecting them to behave differently.

Perhaps you anticipated that they would buy or behave as *you* would have in the same situation? You thought the prospect was primed to purchase. Maybe based on *your* interpretation of the project's goals and team's operating principles, you automatically supposed that they would react as (you) expected. You *had* evaluated these situations but might not have considered certain tacit assumptions on your part, and their implications.

You might not have thought or asked enough to understand your prospect's concerns, specific issues, or distractions. You might not have considered your team members' different agendas and how each person might respond based on their previous behaviors. Moreover, even if most people had bought into the vision and methodology and embraced the culture of the team, each person thinks and reacts in their own way and applies their own interpretations.

Not anticipating your potential buyers' or coworkers' possible responses sufficiently is disadvantageous. Preparing for all likely scenarios so that no one has to backtrack, sidestep, reconfigure, or waste energy is important. Otherwise, how can you optimally respond and convert potential buyers, collaborate with colleagues, manage direct reports appropriately, or give your team reasonable guidance and *freedom* to achieve the necessary outcomes?

When working in an empathetic environment, practicing your empathy skills, these miscommunications, misinterpretations, or erroneous assumptions rarely happen. Using empathy effectively, you are more sensitized to others' states of mind and different perspectives, and you are more aware of your tacit assumptions about what others might do. You pay greater attention to their responses in different situations. You ask more questions and listen harder to people's answers. You also have much stronger relationships and are more attuned to how they think and how to communicate, collaborate, and cooperate productively and easily. Sounds easy, right?

The Effort to Connect

"Do as you would be done by" was the phrase I grew up with in England. The Golden Rule, as it is called in the United States, in more modern language is, "Treat others as you would like to be treated yourself." It sounds good, but it only goes so far. Any other person is not *you* and might prefer you to act very differently. In fact, now there is the Platinum Rule: "Treat others as *they* would like to be treated"—which is all about empathy.

It does take more effort. It is far easier to imagine how *you* would feel in someone's place than how *they* think and feel and would like to be treated. Every single person has their own background, context, knowledge base, and language, resulting in a myriad of nuanced, as well as stark, differences to how *you* might react to a particular situation.

If you update your process to include steps focused on orienting yourself towards others and more deeply connecting with their points of view and feelings, you can better understand, predict, influence, manage, and respond to their reactions. This helps you to realize how your sales proposal might need editing or elements of a project might need to be reconfigured to accommodate differing perspectives and ideas, and to refine your work to achieve optimal results.

Countless times as a kid you likely went through the same process with one of your parents when preparing to ask for permission for something. Or maybe this is currently the norm with your partner as you navigate your different desires and potential ways forwards. Rare is the moment going into a delicate negotiation with a family member or spouse that you have not given thought to how they will react. To be fair, you know them so well that you have endless examples of how they have responded in similar situations, helping you to empathize as you prepare your proposal, pitch your voice, fix your smile, couch your words, and be ready to preempt anticipated counters!

What you typically do not have in sales situations or discussions with coworkers is the same depth of knowledge and history. Without this data, you can easily miss connecting well with the other person's point of view. It takes deliberate effort to orient yourself to their way of thinking, purposefully gather more information, and tap into their experience. Only then is it feasible to assess properly their possible responses to your proposal.

Empathy Is "How"

We typically think about *what* we need to get done, not *how*. These days the "how" matters more than ever. Traditional command-and-control leaders ordered people to do things without engaging them, without seeking their input or buy-in. Issuing those demands was easy—but how have you felt receiving such commands yourself? Few will be surprised to read that research shows authoritative leadership behaviors are detrimental to psychological safety.[1]

Leadership styles have been changing over the past decade to become more empathetic, and managers are doing more to engage their whole teams inclusively. Recognizing the positive effect of greater autonomy, leaders now give fewer one-way directives and are shifting to more collaborative approaches. They are transitioning to oversight roles and coaching methods as responsibility is shared more widely and contributions are solicited to meet faster-paced business demands.

Placid Jover, Vice President of Human Resources for Latin America at Unilever, one of the world's largest consumer goods companies, explained that in his company, when people are reviewed for their performance, they are evaluated not only on *what* they have achieved, but on *how* they did it. "It is important to pay attention to goal achievement as well as how everyone contributed to the success of the team. We also check people's progress on their personal development. We bring a holistic picture of the individual. It is so important that context is taken into account. We also gather feedback and insights to inform decision-making. Our intention is to be consistent, balance managerial judgment with facts, and really own the talent agenda beyond our own teams."[2]

The "how" of management now encompasses several dimensions: ensuring everyone feels included in discussions, soliciting and listening to all opinions, and including more varied inputs in conversations. Our youngest market entrants, in particular, seek out leaders with this management mindset. Research found that the engagement and job satisfaction of US workers aged twenty-one to thirty-four was positively impacted when they were treated with respect.[3] These workers are particularly sensitized, having felt the brunt of the pandemic. Unemployment of US workers sixteen to twenty-four years old rose from 8.4 percent to 24.4 percent from spring 2019 to spring 2020, while unemployment of workers over twenty-five only rose from 2.8 percent to 11.3 percent.[4] In Spain, youth unemployment reached almost 40 percent in 2020, while general unemployment only reached a maximum of 16.3 percent.[5]

How can you best make empathy a key part of how you lead, manage, and interact with people? Start by recognizing the natural empathy you exercise all the time in your family life and interactions with friends, where these steps happen quickly, intuitively, and subconsciously already. The next step is to integrate these same behaviors in your work routines deliberately, make a purposeful strategic mindset shift, and employ tactical habits to move the weight of your attention towards others and away from yourself.

To empathize well while engaging with someone, until you have met them a number of times, you must do prep work, specific practices during the interaction, and thoughtful follow-up afterwards—whether they are an external contact or a colleague at your company. Empathy requires a reasonable amount of research, engaged listening, thoughtful questioning, keen observation, and careful—not presumptive—synthesis. All in all, quite a bit of detective work! How else could you reasonably imagine what another person might be thinking and develop a textured understanding of their professional mindset and opinions, without getting some information about their context and background?

With this data, the benefits are substantial and all your interactions with the person are easier—your efforts are long-lasting and simultaneously deepen your relationship and connection with them. The subsections below describe a simple process for integrating empathy into your work practices to establish new habits. Part III describes when, where, and in which areas you can be practicing your empathy skills.

Empathy Profiles

Shifting the emphasis away from yourself and towards others in a two-way dialogue or group discussion, you benefit from understanding more about the people you are dealing with and gathering, and even logging, details to create a profile for each person. The more you appreciate, can talk to, and connect with another, the easier you can empathize—understand how they think and feel about a situation—and so can respond more in tune with them. They, in turn, feel understood and can more easily reciprocate the connection, leading to better subsequent actions and outcomes.

However you wish to register details—to memory, in shorthand, or in notes—over time you can build up profiles for the people you work closely with outside and inside your organization. The objective is to amass useful information that can be shared in context to foster comfortable conditions and a better connection with their point of view.

Chatting about topics of mutual interest and recognizing common ground, shared stories, and anecdotes are instrumental in developing deeper, more meaningful relationships. This data is also useful for reconnecting at the beginning of a meeting, reminding you both of how and where you agree and bringing you closer together before any discussion starts. Revisiting previously established friendship and familiarity quickly generates feelings of psychological safety between you. A sense of comfort and belonging encourages trust to build, promoting easier external cooperation and conversions, as well as internal communication and collaboration. Personal details to discover include

- whether they have a partner or spouse, or children, parents, or any pets they care for;

- their hobbies, pastimes, and passions outside work;

- their favorite sports team or fitness routine; and

- their favorite current TV show or recent binge-watched series.

These specifics provide a more textured multidimensional picture of the person and help you understand better what makes them tick. You can also find out what excites, bothers, stresses, impassions, and worries them. These are key emotions to identify in a professional setting, when reviewing a matter with them, so that you can interpret their reactions correctly and facilitate the most productive conversations. Professional details to find out encompass

- what they care most about relating to their company's mission and business;

- what they enjoy most about their work;

- what their strengths and key skills are;

- whether they are big-picture or detail-oriented; and

- whether they are more often persuaded by data or stories.

This data also informs your understanding of the person within their or your organization and how they relate to the business. Anna Persin, Co-founder and former Managing

Director of Holker Watkin Limited, a recruiting firm in the United Kingdom, explained how recruiters compile textured profiles to get a substantive read of each promising candidate, often using comparisons and contrasts to build the best composite of them.[6]

In a similar way, you can develop a sense of how someone views their role and responsibilities, how they conduct themselves, and how they accomplish their goals. Internally, a clear definition about how differently and similarly another sees certain aspects in comparison to how you or coworkers do can help you. Furthermore, insights about how and where you align are useful, as these factors likely determine how another relates to and interacts with you.

Especially when there is a critical matter to be discussed, knowing as much as possible about how the other person views a particular project prior to a conversation is invaluable. This might involve reaching out to colleagues of theirs you know to get a better grasp of their position. If your clear intention is to achieve the best overall outcome based on a greater understanding of their point of view, their coworkers should be happy to share some relevant insights with you. However, take note: if they trust you with the information, your reciprocal behavior is important.

Before you interact with someone, assess their individual "baseline": how do they *usually* show up, interact, and react? What is their normal manner; voice tone, speed, and pitch; energy level; sitting position; email response time; and contribution frequency? How do they generally show dissatisfaction, frustration, anger, or concern on their faces and in their manner? Understanding their usual demeanor, you can monitor the progress of a discussion and take Empathetic Action if necessary.

"You only wear the cat filter in meetings when you're having a tough day... What's up, Alex?"

EXERCISE 1: Develop a baseline understanding of the "normal operating mode" for two people you work with—ideally one external partner or vendor and one colleague. Consider their typical behaviors and reactions, such as the following:

- What are their facial expressions for different emotions?

- How much and how confidently do they typically contribute in a meeting?

- How quickly and with what level of detail do they usually respond in email exchanges?

- What is their typical voice energy level, tone, and pitch?

These are a few key aspects. A more comprehensive list is available at empathyworks.online.

With this information, you can remark where they deviate from their typical baseline demeanor. If you note when reactions differ and what causes the change, you can decide how best to respond, asking additional questions or even changing tack to move the discussion forwards productively.

For any meeting—big and small—it is worth preparing ahead of time by thinking about the other person's or people's perspectives: their agenda, potential approach, how they feel about the meeting topic. Consider as well, however the discussion may evolve, and absorbing all participants' inputs, how people may be influenced or convinced. For more important issues and decisions, no doubt you do this already. However, your working life is driven forwards incrementally by numerous daily spoken and written exchanges and micro-meetings, which also benefit from empathetic consideration before interactions begin. As you integrate empathy pervasively, these steps will feel less contrived and become second nature, especially as your comprehension of each external and internal community member builds.

To integrate empathy as you shift your focus to "them," considering the three empathy steps—THINK, FEEL, ACT— orients and paces your actions as you approach and process any interaction. With reasonable data in hand, it is beneficial to recognize how and where empathy matters during the three phases of any encounter: (1) the opening preamble; (2) the live interaction; and (3) the follow-up. The main elements are described below for each phase, and a detailed worksheet is accessible online at empathyworks.online.

I. THE OPENING PREAMBLE: Your immediate goal at the start of the exchange is for both of you quickly to feel at ease, creating a safe environment that allows for productive discussion. Your opener optimally sets the tone with a friendly personal inquiry, (re-)establishes a connection, and attempts to discover their state of mind in case a heightened emotional level needs extended time to dissipate. You may find it easiest to figure out what to say ahead of time to be well prepared. Ideally, this preamble lasts until their voice and body language changes as they become more relaxed with you.

During this initial phase, you will benefit from revealing personal common ground and experiences, as well as demonstrating your open-minded approach to the discussion before sharing previously identified areas of agreement on business issues. All these actions facilitate reciprocal empathetic exchanges, encouraging development of trust-based relationships and mutual understanding of each other's perspectives and responses.

2. THE LIVE INTERACTION: Having fostered a beneficial foundation, move on to the topic to be discussed, initially emphasizing aspects you concur on—so you start on the same side of the table, where your thinking is aligned. This approach improves your capacities to empathize and understand each other's points of view and reactions, helping uncover possible additional and adjacent areas of agreement before you tackle any points of discord. Your earlier demonstration of an open-minded and inclusive attitude, manifestly empathizing with them, hopefully encourages mirrored responses from them, prompting both parties to look for creative solutions.

Clarity is critical to confirm you understand their meaning before you respond, identifying carefully what elements need more exploration, analysis, and debate. If you ask thoughtful questions and draw out their reasoning, you can recognize their point of view more clearly and uncover—possibly incorrect and problematic—tacit assumptions on either side that were detracting from constructive dialogue. At the same time, these exchanges demonstrate your interest in their perspective.

Empathy also involves stepping away from your own reactions and judgments, instead concentrating on connecting with their reasoning and emotional responses, especially when theirs differ from yours. Recalling their baseline manner, observing their tone and expression, you are alert to negative anomalies that might warrant specific attention to facilitate productive progress. Your Empathetic Action might be sharing more data, reframing the issue, using a different approach, or proposing you take a brief ("bio") break.

In preparation for launching into areas where the two of you are not aligned, a beneficial tactic is to reaffirm your relationship, engaging mutually enjoyed feelings of trust that bridge any gaps between you. As you move further away from areas of agreement, try revisiting commonalities and aligned perspectives to support positive attitudes towards each other's views. As you iterate in circles of empathetic discussion, you both stimulate more feelings of trust and potential acceptance.

EXERCISE 2: As you engage in discussion—whether in person or on video call—practice these behaviors to integrate empathy:

- Lean in physically: Proximity and alertness show you are paying attention to what they say. Yes, moving in closer to your screen or leaning away *is* noticeable.

- React visibly: Motions like nodding are important indicators that you are listening. These are absorbed mostly subconsciously by the person speaking.

- Reassure vocally: Audible affirmation, giving quiet comments while they speak, saying, "Yes, I see," and, "Ok, got it," confirms your interest in what they are saying and encourages the person to keep talking and sharing more information.

- Ask open questions: Specific and inviting inquiries reaffirm your concern as well as support more valuable understanding. Examples might be, "How else has that issue affected you?" and, "How have you been trying to deal with this problem so far?"

- Restate their comments: To verify your understanding, rephrasing what they say is important, while it also confirms you are listening and committed to understanding the issue fully. You might say, "By that, do you mean _____?" or, "Did I understand what you meant correctly, that _____?"

- Validate their perspective: Appreciating their experience shows respect and concern, even if you do not share their point of view. Empathizing does not mean you agree. For instance, you can say, "Yes, that sounds like a challenging situation," or, "Yes, you have been making significant changes."

These actions work when they are authentic: when you are speaking with genuine interest in the person and their issues, they open up to share more details. Disingenuous overtures are perceived quickly, whether consciously or not, and the person is likely to feel uncomfortable or hesitant and stop sharing. Without understanding the specifics and nuances, you will have a hard time conducting a fruitful meeting that produces a useful outcome.

Did your new efforts and attention work? Did you find some things worked better than others? Did you notice if certain activities were more effective with particular people? Notice and benefit from the learning, logging the practices that you can make habitual to continue to improve your conversations and collaborations.

Few meetings follow a linear, logical path with defined sequential stages, so adapting seamlessly to the cadence and direction of the conversation is key. Using empathy, you can guide the discussion back to cover all previously defined essential elements and confirm that everyone feels included, because they have had an opportunity to contribute, before deriving any conclusions and wrapping up the meeting.

3. THE FOLLOW-UP: Practicing empathy means making it about "them" in every interaction—synchronous or asynchronous; visual, audio, or written. After any live exchange, integrate your next steps with the same habits as you correspond to confirm meeting outcomes and make subsequent progress:

- Re-establish connection.
- Deepen bonds.
- Reaffirm agreement.
- Ask questions.
- Confirm understanding.
- Validate views.
- Withhold judgments.
- Incorporate inputs.

Now to apply and practice empathy within the business environment, to create competitive advantage for your company. A human-centric orientation throughout your ecosystem ensures your organization is set up for sustainable growth, working closely together, through our liminal environment.

Empathy Takeaways

- Investing additional initial effort and attention to empathize with someone enables you to understand and connect with them more deeply.

- The ends *and* the means matter for achieving our work goals—"how" we do it and treat people along the way, taking a holistic and humanistic approach.

- Develop a profile for each person you work with using empathy to recognize their unique characteristics, where you have commonalities, and what their "normal operating mode" is.

- For any interpersonal exchange—video, audio, or written—attention to preparation, opening preamble, live interaction, and follow-up improves your relationships and outcomes.

6

Showing Empathy Works

LOVE THEORY, but I am also a very practical person. My intention for this book is to get practical and show you how empathy works in a meaningful way. My objective is to support your making empathy real in your work and at your company, and the way that will happen is by integrating empathy, strategically, into everything you do and everyone does—throughout your ecosystem, your workforce, and, ultimately, all your actions—by adopting empathy habits. No small order, right? However, I have no doubt whatsoever that empathy is critical for your company's future sustainable success.

Habits are highly personal. What characterizes yours? Do you generally resist or embrace habits? Is your daily life streamed with routines? Have you noticed habits you have established and maintained more easily than others that were repeatedly launched with gusto, only to slope off disappointingly? Assessing these elements, you can figure out how easily you start and maintain new habits in your working life.

Being deliberate and particular about the best process for you is the first step. There are principles and practices to apply and people to rally to support the establishment of your empathy efforts. Do not underestimate the need for these catalysts, boosts, guard rails, and cheerleaders, no matter how much enthusiasm or conviction you have or how much you recognize the benefits of incorporating empathy practices.

Scientifically speaking, starting a new habit requires exerting energy to forge a new pathway across your brain's network of synapses, breaking activity away from the usual routes, which offer less resistance to energy flow. It is your *committed* executed repetition of the new sequence of thoughts and actions that wears down a preferential route across a new series of synapse nodes to become the habitual course of action—it is your brain's routing of least or low resistance. The cycle of use reduces the effort, and the new sequence becomes the default. It is now automatic—you have created a new habit groove, and going forwards your brain physiologically does not have to think about it!

Ever launched a diet that went astray after a beer or glass of wine with dinner lowered your resistance to having another helping or ordering dessert, after you had been *so* good all day long? I certainly have! Have you made sincere and enthusiastic commitments to complete certain tasks by the end of the day, but somehow other "urgent" matters so often got ahead of them? I'm with you.

When researching habits, and in particular through the studies reported in Charles Duhigg's book *The Power of Habit* and Gretchen Rubin's book *Better Than Before*, I found relative consensus that we each have a finite daily supply of energy dedicated to exerting self-will. This is important to keep in mind for launching your new empathy habits. We are likely to have depleted self-discipline resources when we are tired, at the end of the day or when diverted by some other influence. Incorporating new activities is going to be easiest, with the highest probability of success, if you purposefully allocate a portion of your daily "stock" of self-discipline to keep you on track until you have created your groove with the new habits.

Steps to Success

To ensure empathy permeates your organization as a key value, mindset, and orientation for all your interactions, make micro-moves in sensible steps. If you are toying with going big and bold—*don't do it!* Too often these enthusiastic and desirably heroic leaps fall short, lead to disappointment, and frustrate future progress. Sounds good, feels great out of the gate, but it's very hard to sustain. Taken in small steps, consolidating and confirming adoption as you continue, you can make consistent, compounding progress with empathy. Here are the Seven Steps to Success:

1 **PRACTICE:** Flex those empathy muscles! Chapters of this book include exercises designed to draw out your natural empathy. With indications for where and how you can optimally introduce, augment, or more consistently apply the three empathy steps—THINK, FEEL, and ACT— you can purposefully incorporate more empathy within your work-related activities. Experience (more) empathy in different settings and scenarios at work. Increase your effective practice of empathy skills and witness the compounding effects.

2 **PRIORITIZE:** Once you have felt mental and emotional connections with a few colleagues, you can prioritize where to focus your new empathy habits. Consider where you have the greatest need to improve interactions and

outcomes within your business ecosystem: from potential buyers to coworkers and freelancers; from executives to direct reports and vendors. Assess situations to identify where immediate attention is due. Review the chapters in Part III that explain where, when, and how to apply empathy to cultivate the improvements you want. Pick two or three habits from the Empathy Habits section at the end of the chapters in Part III that address your most pressing concerns, and focus your attention on them.

3 **PAIR:** Identify an activity to trigger your new habit, to facilitate building repeated practice. Coupling the new practice right before (preferably) or after a regular step in your existing routine is recommended. For example, for relationship-building, every time you start a meeting, allocate several minutes to thoughtful checking-in with each attendee. Create a relevant and regular pairing to trigger each new habit.

4 **PARTNER:** Do you have a friend you work out or do yoga with? Is there someone who helps you eat healthily? Perhaps the same person, or specific people, keep you focused on particular goals and hold you accountable. Starting and sustaining work-related habits is no different. Do not attempt this alone! Find a relevant buddy for each new empathy habit, depending on their needs and habits as well, so the association is mutually beneficial.

5 **PLAN:** You need to track your progress to get a dopamine boost of satisfaction with every completed milestone— *check* ✓! Figure out how often you and your buddy reasonably need to monitor slippage and successful sustainability. Create a checklist to help you stay sufficiently aware of your regular achievements.

6 **PATIENCE:** How is it going: after two, four, eight, and twelve weeks? How hard do you still need to think about each habit? Which is on cruise control and which is a little shaky, where you might have missed a few scheduled times over the last two to three weeks? This is normal when establishing a new routine. Have patience with yourself. Different habits typically take hold at different times. Establishing new neural sequences takes initial effort. Check in with your buddy to pinpoint any resistance, distractions, or inconsistencies. Tweak any faltering activities after figuring out what has been disrupting you. It could take more than one or two tweaks to get it right after making a new plan to test and track it.

7 **PROGRESS:** You picked and paired your priority habits, and you determined a schedule with a partner and a plan to track your progress. By the time you are sustaining a couple of new habits with ease, you should find that there are natural synergies, overlapping similarities in your actions, and a compounding effect that brings benefits to other areas of your work. Each new habit will be easier to launch and successfully maintain as you infuse all your work behaviors with empathy, establishing a strategic orientation that supports all your professional needs and goals.

Measuring Empathy

The field of behavioral science really emerged in the United States in the 1950s but has gained most significant attention in the twenty-first century, and more is being discovered every year.[1] Much measurement is qualitative rather than quantitative, which raises eyebrows and issues with some people. Empathy can be challenging to measure directly, such that it has been viewed as a quagmire that few scientists want to wade into. As the value we place on interpersonal skills increases, with more investment and research, better quantitative metrics will surely be developed over the coming years.

However, leading health solutions company CVS Health already measures empathy, especially in pharmacies, prompted by its CMO, Norman de Greve, who told me, "I thought it was going to be really important for us to deliver empathy. And when our colleagues heard we were going to track empathy, they said, 'Thank goodness! You're finally going to track what we thought was important all along.'"[2] At CVS Health, empathy is integrated, Norman noted, in the company's "interaction model that we encourage for our store colleagues, our CARE model: Connect, Ask, Respond, and Empathize. What we see is that people not only are more loyal, they're also more adherent to their medication, which is great for their health."

Marketing, sales, and service software company HubSpot leans into its Culture Code of HEART, which stands for Humble, Empathetic, Adaptable, Remarkable, and Transparent. HubSpot also regularly surveys employees about their happiness and sense of inclusion—which they connect very closely with empathy.[3] They use the survey data to monitor progress and identify potential training needs.

Your company, division, or team can also monitor the impact of empathy. The key is to measure appropriate baseline data that can be compared with after empathetic values, mindsets, and practices start and settle. For your organization, measurement might include tracking the number of suggestions shared among sales team members to assist one another's conversions, employees' sense of belonging, how comfortable people feel speaking up in meetings, and how well supported employees working remotely feel. Find metrics that show how empathy works and produces results that encourage people to start, persevere, and maintain empathy habits. As more employees join in, a network effect compounds people's efforts and multiplies outcomes.

Showing Empathy Works

In 2020, Mary Barra, CEO of General Motors, took a trust-based, human-centric approach and tapped into the individual and combined sense of community and commitment of the company's more than 150,000 employees during the first year of the COVID-19 crisis. She reduced hundreds of words of corporate dress policy down to two words that gave the direction and shared the responsibility: "Dress appropriately." She showed empathy by recognizing that, given more autonomy, people (generally) make reasonable choices. She took the same straightforward approach when devising GM's hybrid work model in May 2021 with another compelling, pithy two-word policy: "Work appropriately."[4] She understands that employees reciprocate when they get more control and accountability.

Yes, the proof is in the pudding. Which is why exercises to experience it yourself set you on your journey of discovery, trial, error, and fine-tuning. The critical kicker is that as you practice, pay attention to the immediate benefits and substantially improved outcomes. You can then put the resulting determination behind the launch and maintenance of empathy habits infused in your work routines and build the momentum you need to make it last.

Part III outlines areas and aspects of your business, describing how a human-centric mindset and approach applies on a daily basis, and how and where empathetic behaviors focused on your prospects, customers, and employees benefit your business and workforce. Specific empathy habits are detailed for each area that can be usefully applied to instill or enhance an overall or particularly focused empathetic approach.

I urge you to do the exercises and start some empathy habits with genuine effort. Sure, I can describe the theory and share numerous compelling stories and anecdotes from other companies, leaders, and managers. However, nothing will convince you more than *you showing yourself* what a difference empathy makes.

When you exercise your empathy skills, you start to recognize how pervasive empathy is as a profound orientation—externally and internally—creating productive work environments and positively influencing behaviors and decisions for your organization, its positioning, and your relationships. Flexible frameworks and open-minded inclusive approaches centered on individuals across your ecosystem, from customers to contractors, will show you empathy really works.

Empathy Takeaways

- Any new habit takes effort to start and sustain until the new series of activities becomes the path of least resistance in your brain.

- Adopt the Seven Steps to Success to launch new empathy habits successfully, so you can quickly experience the profound benefits across all your professional relationships.

- To improve your interactions in areas that are a priority, choose two or three empathy habits from relevant chapters in Part III (or go to empathyworks.online for the master list).

PART II

THE NEW ERA OF WORK: CATALYZED TRANSFORMATION

Empathy is integral to the
new human-centric system.

7

Intervention and Inflection

PEANUT BUTTER makes a fantastic sandwich, is a comfort food, and is a highly nutritious daily staple, especially when food supplies and money are tight. In April 2020, at the height of the first lockdown, Kimmi Wernli, President and Owner of Crazy Richard's Peanut Butter Company, which produces wholesome foods for the whole family, was rallying to play her part in efforts to support food security. The company was focused on ensuring they could keep supermarket shelves stocked with product for their customers who needed it as stockpiling during lockdowns was leaving shelves empty.[1]

They had to adapt for COVID-19 safety protocols, including physical distancing and automating hand-offs. Production was down: they could not fulfill all of their orders because workers in the manufacturing plants needed to be well spaced out, reducing throughput. Fulfillment was down: they could not deliver all of their output, because other steps along the distribution chain were also not able to operate at typical capacity.

However, the companies within their ecosystem were strongly aligned, and everyone along the supply chain pulled together to maximize final outcomes, empathizing with each other's situations. Every company involved absorbed a portion of the shortfall and disruption so that no business took the full burden, while also ensuring as much product as possible arrived in stores and was available for their common, ultimate customer. It was not about fighting for the best deal for any particular business along the chain but collaborating and compromising from beginning to end.

This alignment had been a very purposeful objective of Kimmi's when she took over running the business in 2014.[2] At a senior management group gathering, she explained that the culture of the organization and its values were critically important to her. They took some months to agree and articulate their vision for the business and the values that mattered most to them and became a certified B Corporation, reinforcing these values.

Just as deliberately, she initiated a review of all their vendors and partners—from manufacturing to distribution and retail. If they found that any business was not an ally in achievement of their vision and cultural values, they respectfully parted ways. This direction became a point of contention with more than one of the other company executives, who expressed frustration at the decision to cut ties.

"But why? These are revenue-generating relationships!" one executive exclaimed.

"I understand," Kimmi said. "However, our values connect us more deeply than any contract, more than any terms we agree upon."

The executive was not convinced. "If they don't believe in all the same things we do, does it really matter?"

Kimmi insisted, "I respect your point of view. I am also convinced that this is important, and we are moving forward and ensuring we have business partners who understand who we are, what we want to achieve, and how. Alignment with our vision and values throughout our ecosystem matters and will support our growth and ongoing success."

Kimmi and the executive team reached a consensus, and they moved ahead, parting ways with a few retailers and other relationships along the supply chain. Eventually the senior executive departed as well. Kimmi was disappointed but remained convinced about how best to make sustained progress.

Kimmi's belief and insistence in consistent and congruent values and in empathetic connection and understanding brought her company's ecosystem much closer together during the COVID-19 crisis. Their relationships and sense of allyship helped them all survive during emergency circumstances, including the worst months. Most importantly to her, it also helped them to keep supplying customers with the peanut butter and other products they needed. Kimmi's empathy for her customers' situations and the congruent values and goals throughout her ecosystem enabled everyone involved to work together and fulfill people's urgent needs during crisis conditions.

Dissonance and Discord

Before the proliferation of social media, many of us had not felt too much need to empathize with our customers. We gave them what they wanted. We knew what they wanted. Or we thought we did! Certainly some companies had started paying attention to their prospects' and customers' reactions and experiences. But many businesses were shaken up when customers got a voice across multiple platforms, which they used to give clear feedback about recent purchases. We have had to react, often accelerating the release of new features and functionalities in response to buyers' opinions and posts—which we couldn't ignore if we wanted to!

We have been forced to empathize more. With frank critique about our offerings being public and available, if we didn't listen and respond we could expect fewer conversions, and our competitors could use the same information to their benefit. Instead, more empathetic interactions with our external audiences gave us critical data to create and build our advantage.

Consider also what was required from Kimmi and the rest of the company—as well as those working all along the value chain—to create and distribute their products. Kimmi had made a concerted effort, undergoing a purposeful, strategic project to agree, align, and bring reasonable consistency to the behaviors, approaches, and experiences of people working throughout the company's ecosystem.

In general, businesses optimizing for profits and market share have analyzed how to improve sales results, marketing demand, innovative products, and even customer service. However, executives have not appreciated the extent or potential range of workers' contributions, which could also be optimized and affect results significantly. Companies have been called out on occasion when the public has found out their great customer service is at odds with their treatment of employees. Discord between external and internal behaviors and incongruent customer and employee experiences have been increasingly visible, often deterring existing and prospective buyers.

The Perfect Storm

Workers were also facing compounding challenges as digitization increased the speed, interdependencies, and uncertainty of business developments across our ecosystems.

The perfect storm was brewing at work with a confluence of technological, societal, and economic developments and consequent tensions:

- Increasing numbers of double-income parents and working single mothers were under greater financial strain, struggling without flexibility or accommodation by employers.[3]

- The automation of simple, repeatable tasks had elevated the sophistication of entry-level jobs by three to four years for recent graduates, whose school education was poorly matched with their evolving work requirements and partly irrelevant or obsolete.[4]

- Companies focused on shareholder value were unbundling and phasing out decades-long employment arrangements, benefits, and retirement, so younger employees had started hustling multiple jobs with less or no job security and anticipated no retirement, since numerous national and state pension schemes are underfunded.

- A disconnection was forming between most US Generation Zs, 76 percent of whom in 2018 expected to get promotions in their first year, in line with the new pace and complexity of business, and their bosses, who perceived them as lazy and entitled.[5]

- Younger workers were seeking employers with purpose to give meaning to their work, as well as aligned values and commitment to developing their skills, also attempting to reduce their angst about income insecurity and buttress their series of careers and fragmented work projects.

- Longer life expectancy was reducing the sustainability of retirement and pension savings and causing a variety of discord—with some nations' senior employees seeking to phase out, rather than drop out, of work,[6] while others fought government attempts to postpone retirement.[7]

- Unpredictable marketplace demands and evolving needs for skills were creating a long-term trend of organizations that rely on a smaller core of full-time employees who were flexibly supplemented by contracted short- and long-term workers.

We all have been involved in tense interactions as the terms of our established social contract—the implicit agreed terms of compensation for our employment—have been disintegrating across many countries. The patriarchal organization used to look after us. But by 2019, most employment models were out of date, and employees strained to accommodate their financial, professional, social, and psychological needs.

There has been a growing call for reformed formulae for our economic models, from French socialism to American-style capitalism. A reconfiguration of business—and work-related—dynamics has been needed to update terms for the complexity of conditions of our modern world. The strains have been real and increasingly obvious.

The storm was building.

One step in the right direction was the announcement by the Business Roundtable in August 2019 that the "Purpose of a Corporation" should now be creating *stakeholder* value: "Companies should serve not only their shareholders, but also deliver value to their customers, invest in employees, deal fairly with suppliers and support the communities in which they operate."[8] Signed by the CEOs of almost 200 major US corporations, this statement of purpose was meaningful. Words matter. But it was not pervasive, visible, or actionable enough to assuage the resentments and misunderstandings, to reduce the insecurities and difficulties.

In parallel, the patriarchal model, built upon lop-sided power dynamics and information access, was slowly, inexorably shifting to less patronizing and hierarchical, more mutually beneficial trade-offs and relationships between employers and employees. But we were still in pursuit of a "good job," which assumed that there was a bundle of benefits that came with it.

Laetitia Vitaud, an authority on the Future of Work and author of *Du labeur à l'ouvrage* ("From Graft to Craft" in English), who explores the Future of Work and consumption, posited, "Perhaps we should ask the question, 'What is good work?' which is a difficult question, because there isn't a single answer anymore."[9] We urgently needed a recalibrated social contract with updated and relevant terms between employers and extended talent pools—blended combinations of full- and part-time employees, freelancers, and longer-term contractors.

With numerous studies showing how much employees' treatment and circumstances affect their engagement, productivity, and capacity to be flexible and responsive, more organizations were starting to transition from transactional to experiential approaches. Employer/employee relationships were beginning to mirror deepening customer relationships. Executives at businesses providing competitive customer experiences were turning attention to employees' experiences. But the interplay of increasing, complex forces required a transformation. Incremental shifts would be insufficient; resistance would be too great.

Then the COVID-19 pandemic struck.

The crisis did not *cause* the business and work transformation already underway, primarily generated by technology developments and implementations, although these were accelerated. However, the ensuing turbulence became a calamitous intervention catalyzing a rare period of inflection. Our dramatic and prolonged, self-inflicted, and constricted conditions exposed and confronted us with new realities, possibilities, opportunities, and necessities.

"The whole process of work dramatically changed, particularly with the arrival of artificial intelligence and the Fourth Industrial Revolution more broadly. That's all been accelerated by five to ten years. Something we could have adjusted to more incrementally is now requiring much more rapid adaptation. The pain of that disruption is going to be much more intense and the need to act quickly much greater," Matthew Bishop, former Business Editor of the *Economist* and author of *The Future of Jobs: The Great Mismatch*, told me.[10]

The great disparity in attitudes towards customers and employees decreased dramatically when the pandemic struck. People working from home or on the frontline experienced relatable stressors the world over, increasing our ability to empathize with customers and colleagues alike. Transactional attitudes and approaches became heartless at worst and ineffective at best.

After the severely disruptive successive waves of the pandemic, the scars and sensibilities of our experiences remain with us, as the customers and employees who we all are. The tragedy and turbulence of the pandemic confronted us and stimulated more meaningful and expanded adoption of empathetic, experiential methods and management styles, which has had a profoundly beneficial effect, in my opinion.

With a Human Lens

The structural disruption is significant, systemic, and global, depending to some degree on the digitalization levels of nations' private and public sectors, and it is shaking up our business worlds. The reweighted emphasis, with a greater perceived value of workers, anticipates the evolution of a more balanced social contract between employers and employees. While you do not have to participate in crafting new terms at higher levels, you are unavoidably deeply involved in the changes affecting your own ecosystem.

The new powerfully positive orientation for optimization of your organization and business is human-centric. The new strategic approach to create competitive advantage is framed by and focused on customers' *and* employees' experiences. These complementary halves of your business core, integrated with operations, mutually reinforce each other through common, consistent behaviors. "Things are much more transparent and available because of the digital space and because things change so rapidly that you need to have a set of values and you need to have much more centricity towards both your consumers and your employees," said Norman de Greve.[11]

Neil Bedwell, Founding Partner of Change Marketing agency LOCAL, uses the clear visual of an infinity loop to illustrate the impactful beneficial interplay that he believes exists between external and internal corporate human experiences.[12] Manifesting his conviction, Neil applies his expertise in traditional, externally focused consumer marketing to craft internally focused, empathetic employee communications to effect meaningful change within organizations.

What does this experiential emphasis mean for your company? Are your company's employees focused on serving your potential and existing customers? How tuned in are your sales teams to prospects' issues and what clients are going through? How consistent is treatment of customers and employees? Are employees' experiences helping or hindering their full participation? How much effort do leaders put into understanding and supporting employees' individual needs?

Do workers get the tools and training they need with current technologies to be effective in their jobs? How prepared do you feel your organization is for future business conditions?

Competitive advantage in the new, digitally driven business environment can be established and maintained through proactive, strategic transformation to the human-focused era of work. When your organization fully adopts this emphasis—integrating empathy as a value and standard orientation for all behaviors—sustainable growth and desired outcomes for your business are achievable. As Muriel Clauson, Co-founder of Anthill, stated unequivocally, "Technology actually won't be a real differentiator in the future, it will be people."[13]

With empathetic and inclusive alignment of all divisions, as well as all along your supply chain, leaders can foster better understanding, communication, and collaboration. They can better support the people, internally and throughout the ecosystem, who are responsible for generating the results—whether developing, providing, or purchasing your offering.

Some transformation is unavoidable simply to stay in business, but this concentration and conversion is no small feat, I admit freely. No doubt, you are also aware because you have already started aspects of the transition: perhaps increasing focus on customers before 2020, infusing work interactions with more empathy since the start of the pandemic, or adapting work arrangements to be more flexible. I imagine you have experienced the benefits of some changes, but that some need tweaks and refinements, and others require a rethink, redesign, and reboot. That is to be expected with such a major, much-needed overhaul.

You're on it. Potentially without being aware of the full picture, your work in progress, in motion, is to reconfigure an integrated system that is flexible and responsive enough, and that provides you with sufficient competitive advantage for your business growth and sustainable success. Then you can achieve the desired complementary and mutually reinforcing strategic benefits in customer relationships and conversions, as well as in employee engagement, responsiveness, and retention.

These makeover shifts, highlighting empathy to nurture your expansive business environment and behaviors, support and reinforce everyone's efforts. The key is to be strategic, deliberate, and consistent in elevating the human factor across all your company's plans, decisions, and activities. Applying a systematic and comprehensive approach, you can achieve the necessary transformation for your company, building upon and benefiting from whatever adaptations and advances you have made thus far.

Empathy Takeaways

- Economic and employment circumstances were under increasing strain prior to the COVID-19 pandemic.

- Crisis conditions catalyzed the arrival of Future-of-Work environments and generated a period of inflection, which supports necessary transformation.

- Confluent forces stimulating an update to the social contract are rebalancing the employer/employee equation.

- Competitive advantage in our tech-driven world is human-centric—putting critical emphasis on customers' and employees' experiences.

8

The Human-centric System

"COMPANIES THAT are succeeding are the ones which have a much deeper understanding and relatedness to both their employees and their consumers," observed Norman de Greve.[1] To facilitate congruent and coordinated design and execution throughout your ecosystem, the next step is to ensure orientation of everyone's focus on the Customer Journey.

Customer Journey

To start with, have you defined your optimal customer? Who are they? Is their profile up to date? Does everyone in the company know and have the same clear mental image of who this person or business is? Do they know about their current circumstances, how they are feeling, or what they dealing with?

If not, the challenge, and potential conflict, is divergent interpretations of these potential customers' needs that different areas of your organization are trying to satisfy. Small initial differences can later result in chasms of understanding that may be completely hidden, as everyone *assumes* they are focused on serving the same prospect or customer and trying to comprehend the world from their perspective and their experiences. Alignment about the key customer profile is essential, even more so now, when the landscape and behaviors are evolving, sometimes in unexpected ways.

Directing every division towards identified and defined target customers becomes central to achieving your purpose *and* profits. Everyone can then agree on an appropriate integrated, systematic approach, as well as the operational steps and elements involved to seek, sell, serve, and support your customers. This coordination aligns all employees towards the same agreed goals, promoting cooperation and cross-disciplinary problem-solving, as well as connecting people with the meaning of their work, which magnifies their efforts. Focusing on your customer is both strategic and tactical for achieving success.

Appropriate priorities and trade-offs can only be assessed properly when interrelated departments similarly comprehend customers' priorities, issues, and deal breakers, to determine the optimal—and realistically achievable—strategies and tactics. Can you imagine the kind of discord that could be generated without alignment throughout the rest of the organization?

From the CEO to frontline employees, using empathy all along the Customer Journey is essential for creating, enhancing, and maintaining a competitive edge. Your business depends on *multidimensional and coordinated* understanding of your prospects and customers:

- CREATION: How quickly are customers' comments incorporated into product or service updates based on current, empathetic understanding of your target audience(s)?

- AWARENESS: How well do marketing campaigns intersect with high-probability prospects and use current customers' feedback to stimulate relevant positive connections with your brand?

- DISTRIBUTION: Are operations teams working with account teams to refine the optimal way to deliver or disseminate your offering based on existing customers' current habits?

- CONSIDERATION: Do sales reps have all the data they need to be most empathetic in conversations with prospects, including current clients' typical issues and usage insights?

- ACQUISITION: Are sales teams collaborating—sharing winning strategies and tactics with each other—to best tune in to potential buyers' situations and convert target prospects?

- EXPERIENCE: Do account teams build strong, empathy-based relationships while serving clients so clients hear about relevant developments and upsell opportunities early?

- ADVOCACY: Are strong personal, product/service, and brand connections with customers encouraging loyalty and referrals to improve business results?

Deloitte's "2022 Global Marketing Trends" research revealed that "the highest growing brands (those with 10 percent higher annual revenue growth) are comprehensively addressing the entire customer experience—from activating an enterprise-wide purpose to overhauling customer data strategies. This requires collaboration across all functions of the organization, with leaders working together to create 360-degree engagement encompassing people, data, and experiences."[2]

EXERCISE 1: Keeping customers' perspectives and experiences top of mind, follow your company's Customer Journey, assessing for current conditions and implemented technologies, and inviting all business units to share inputs from areas they touch. Discuss medium-term possible permutations, including

- greater collaboration in areas of overlap;
- more data sharing to augment approaches; and
- new available technologies that could improve operations, processes, and outcomes—especially if competitors are implementing any.

Notice beneficial modifications resulting from these conversations.

All operational sectors are key players, working closely together to find, serve, and sustain your customers effectively. These new circumstances require the Human Resources and Information Technology divisions now to have C-suite-level *strategic* representation.

- HUMAN RESOURCES. The human focus that encompasses employees, too, requires integrating Human Resources into influential activities and messaging relating to culture and operations to ensure congruent and consistent attitudes, approaches, and treatment of customers *and* workers. What other division at your company has the oversight, integrated presence, and ability to coordinate and track these critical efforts?

- INFORMATION TECHNOLOGY. The digital impetus of business drives a necessary mindset shift, embedding technology's role in your company's competitive positioning. Assessing individual steps as well as the integrated flow and hand-offs along the Customer Journey, everyone needs to collaborate on optimal methods to serve your buyers, both potential and existing. The importance of selecting, adopting, and optimizing appropriate technology platforms, applications, and communications channels gives your IT department a strategic, rather than tactically functional, role.

Employee Journey

The complementary "yin" to the Customer Journey's "yang" is the Employee Journey, which comprises all workers' activities and interactions, manifesting a symbiotic relationship through consistent treatment of everyone involved. Just as concentrating on the Customer Journey facilitates integrated efforts by all divisions on prospective and existing customers' experiences, so strategic emphasis on the Employee Journey generates coordinated, coherent, and supportive employee experiences. Note also that, as work arrangements evolve, with employers and employees exploring more options, the experiences of non-employee workers also become relevant for attention and strategic alignment to support their productive contributions.

From outreach to onboarding, recruiting to retention, the Employee Journey encompasses the environment, why, who, what, where, when, and how of each person's working life:

- WHY: The organization's purpose, mission, and vision, which give meaning to work, are supported by a trust-based, inclusive cultural environment and aligned values.

- WHO: All employees are welcomed and valued; experiences include freelancers and contractors participating in the total talent pool.

- WHAT: Workflow is identified, defined, and (re)designed to be flexible; tasks are assigned in alignment with workers' strengths and skills, which are intentionally developed over time.

- WHERE: Location options enhance workers' performance, improve outcomes with a "location independent" approach, and provide inclusive and equitable access, support, training, and promotion.

- WHEN: Scheduling options help optimize engagement; management fosters employees' regular skills updates and supports non-linear career progression.

- HOW: Nurturing self-awareness and trusting relationships, leadership models transparent and open-minded interactions, enabling effective collaboration and responsive, results-focused work.

EXERCISE 2: In preparation for a deep dive, map out your company's current Employee Journey, detailing all the relevant steps from first outreach to final contact. Consider what aspects and milestone moments you believe your company handles well, as well as others where more empathy could support better employee experiences. Involve other departments in developing a realistic overview of a worker's trajectory, including non-employees who also participate in value creation.

To implement an effective Employee Journey for your organization that generates successful customer experiences all along your Customer Journey, while also engaging and supporting your workforce, you need to infuse and integrate empathy throughout. Part III of this book discusses in much detail the Employee Journey and where to focus your energies when applying empathy. A few particular areas receive greater attention because of their disproportionate influence on employees and your whole ecosystem, enabling your company to create and maintain a meaningful competitive advantage. These are:

- NEW WORK MODELS: explaining the seismic shift in workers' perspectives, attitudes, and desired arrangements, and ways to implement more complex models effectively

- CULTURE: emphasizing the fundamental tenets and values that guide workers' actions and foster positive and productive individual and team experiences

- THE CONTEMPORARY WORKER: embracing the uniqueness of each individual and the enablement of their fullest contributions

- EXPERIENTIAL ELEMENTS: following employees' paths to, around, and beyond your company and expanding upon additional elements to pay attention to

- SALES: driving your revenues by supporting all employees' outward-facing interactions with greater use of empathy

- LEADERSHIP: updating methods and styles by delegating more, soliciting widespread inputs, offering greater flexibility, and transitioning to customized, coaching-based oversight

- TEAMWORK: acknowledging empathy's beneficial effect on collaboration and cooperation for employee groups tasked with complex problem-solving, especially during uncertain times

We can step back and consider how best to craft our pathways forwards, with different perspectives and possible approaches, to be competent and successful in a digitized new era of work. To effect transformational change, a design-thinking approach embedded with human-centric, empathetic sensibilities will allow you to foster suitable, relevant new internal work interactions, situations, and settings for your Employee Journey.

Systematic Empathy

Handelsbanken is a 150-year-old multinational bank operating across Europe and in the United Kingdom. Mikael Sorensen, CEO of Handelsbanken UK, shared the company's human-centric approach: "If you take good care of your staff and your customers, that will also benefit other stakeholders in the bank, both your shareholders and regulators and society in general."[3] As both a value and a key element of critical interpersonal skillsets, empathy has become a strategic necessity at the core of your ecosystem, as daily operations and management practices become more heavily reliant on human interactions. Business arrangements with partners and suppliers now include stronger alliances and greater integration to navigate uncertainties together and make joint bets on the future.

Our actions across our own ecosystem matter during times of transformation. Our choices affect others across the entire supply chain and throughout the extended community of interrelated players. These dependencies have likely been highlighted for you since the pandemic began, as supply chains suffered numerous disruptions, including insufficient and delayed deliveries of raw materials and components, causing breaks in production and inventories to be depleted. Relationships with your vendors and possible sales intermediaries were undoubtedly strained, but they were also likely cemented as aligned interests and empathetic mutual understanding deepened trusting cooperation.

Molly Kellogg, CEO of Hubbard-Hall, a 170-year-old chemical distributor and specialty chemical manufacturer, discussed the issues affecting the business, their customers, and their suppliers in August 2021. "Happily, there is a high level of real empathy in the situation—in talking to my customers and suppliers and listening to my salespeople, everyone is really trying to help one another get through an unprecedented time."[4]

Organizations in the same ecosystem benefit from discussing future scenarios and possibilities, getting a deeper understanding of each other's situations, risks, future choices, opportunities, and challenges. Have any senior executives considered or developed this approach yet? What vendor or client relationship could you develop further to improve business adaptability and resilience?

Similarly, vendors and clients might have needed to modify parts of their value chain since March 2020 because of changes in circumstances, operating practices, target customers, and newly implemented technologies. If it has not already been done, an empathetic analysis of your entire business ecosystem is a worthwhile exercise, especially noticing modifications that have occurred since the pandemic began. How your business has adjusted might be affecting how to mutually optimize operating flow with other companies. Possible changes in the companies you work with might be relevant, if you are now not well aligned values-wise and operationally.

Supply chain alignment and shared values become all the more evident if shifting targets or strategies cause divergences. Operations may continue to be in flux along your supply chain as companies absorb and adapt to new realities, from disruption to diversification. Change is a constant now, and the flexible and adaptive mindset needed to understand and meet your clients' businesses' needs is applicable along the supply chain as well.

We have all been adapting to evolving conditions that have had extensive ripple effects potentially impacting everyone's revenues and future growth possibilities. It benefits us all to recognize and be more attuned empathetically to our partners' and clients' changes and challenges. Then, we can coordinate adjustments and facilitate smooth operations and service as much as possible across our ecosystems, just as Kimmi Wernli did. United by a cohesive Employee Journey, the team at Crazy Richard's Peanut Butter could be effective, intently focused on the Customer Journey to make sure everyone got their delicious wholesome products!

Empathy Takeaways

- The human-centric system comprises the symbiotic, complementary, and mutually reinforcing Customer Journey and Employee Journey.

- The Customer Journey tracks, end to end, how your company attracts, engages, relates, converts, and provides your offering to prospects and customers.

- The Employee Journey maps the worker's path from the start—to, through, and back to your organization—in employee and non-employee work arrangements.

- Coherent orientation means integrating and elevating empathy as a core value, mindset, and skill throughout your ecosystem.

PART III

THE EMPLOYEE JOURNEY: INTEGRATING EMPATHY

Empathy is the key
to your competitive
advantage in the
new era of work.

9

New Work Models
Adapting for Remote Work Options

Y ES, THE Digital Genie is out of the bottle, causing all kinds of multidimensional change! New work models are disruptive—but necessary—adaptations for organizations to be adequately responsive. They are not easy to implement. I agree, wholeheartedly. But offering new options is both an unavoidable consequence of our new circumstances and critical for your business to adopt and for employees to keep going, honing, and refining. Yes, the new capacities of your employees are worth the fits and starts, the leaps forwards and setbacks, the gathering and dispersing, the confusion and clarity, and the iterations and eventual exaltations.

To be fair, it took a lingering multi-year global pandemic to prove that rigid work restrictions—whether forced to be office-based or locked down at home—do not allow people do their best work. "Aha!" moments resonated around the world when diehard proponents of office working found that productivity did not drop off a cliff when millions of employees were sent home to work.

Yet still, in early summer 2021, the CEO of a major financial institution told me the "Digital Genie *is* going back in the bottle" as everyone was called back to the office. He emphatically declared that eighteen months from then, workplaces would look very similar to how they had pre-pandemic. I respectfully shared my belief that this would not be the case. As the conversation continued, his stance seemed tactical as we agreed more than we did not. Deeply empathetic in service of the firm's clients, he was also well attuned to new employee demands and what adjustments might become appropriate to maintain competitive advantage.

"He refuses to go back in!"

Pockets of resistance or regression remain. These are natural. Fear and inertia are the two most powerful causes of resistance to change. Plus, there is a strong desire for familiarity and stability—to erase the memories of the uncertainties and turmoil of the pandemic—which new working models cannot offer quickly. Some companies, executives, and managers tried to revert to pre-pandemic habits. They made coworkers return to the office, embracing comfortable old routines. Burdened by the weight of previous practices, they were unwilling or unable to build momentum and make rather complicated progress to higher-functioning, more adaptive work models. Some were also quick to point out potential inequities—what about factory workers and others who *had* to work on-site?

Meanwhile, you are convinced of the need, viability, and suitability of flexible working models. Now you want to improve the effectiveness of the model implemented at your organization. You would also benefit from an overall approach that synchronizes with how you are managing your business, division, or team, wherever they want or have to work. Indeed, empathy is certainly the core value at the heart of any viable workplace flexibility options you offer at your company, as well as being the key skill to practice to make the model work—for every executive, leader, and employee.

Let's be clear first. "Workplace flexibility" is the important umbrella term for what you are likely aiming to achieve: a combination of configurations geared to enable each person to do their best work. Consider anything other than nine-to-five, five days a week at a company site, such as these options:

- forty-hour four-day workweeks
- all company-site-based work, with shifted hours
- all non-company-site-based work at one or more non-company-site locations

- days and hours split between the company site and home or other locations
- job or function sharing
- home office plus client sites only

When we lean into this array of choices, we all give and get much more out of work.

In spring 2021, Cary Bruce, Senior Vice President and General Manager at EBSCO Information Services, the leading provider of research databases, e-journals, magazine subscriptions, ebooks, and discovery service to libraries of all kinds, was heading up a multinational operational division and responsible for over 500 people in eleven offices across Europe and South Africa. He was triaging many challenges: the disruption of the pandemic, the impact of accelerated digitalization upon the company's core business model, and developing a new work model for his entire group. Some of the decade-plus-long office leases were coming up for renewal. Logically prompted by enormous increases looming with these renewals, Cary took a strategic approach and developed a new configuration. The design needed to accommodate, as far as possible, a particular locale's individuals and group; their optimal working profiles, team needs, and combined preferences; and current and anticipated business needs.[1]

During the exploration process, together with his management and HR team, he considered the perspectives, preferences, work content, and circumstances of employees in different job categories. With employee feedback, he assessed who benefited from in-person and virtual sparring partners for their collaboration projects, and who worked more independently, including those with administrative or customer service tasks. Cary reflected upon the working profiles of individuals and how to optimize for those who performed best in more structured settings and for others who easily adapted to more innovative or flexible learning environments. He had developed strong relationships with employees over the years and gathered an understanding of the local dynamics across national cultures and the office network. Connecting during and after work and going for friendly dinners when traveling regularly around his region of responsibility, on each trip Cary purposefully spent a couple of days getting to know key leaders. However, numerous exchanges were still necessary to collect enough granular data from employees to craft a suitable customized, long-term framework.

After carefully reviewing the purpose and plan for each of his division's eleven offices, Cary decided that—for now at least—having some physical location to meet in person was beneficial for their division, especially for onboarding new recruits. Starting new jobs off with dedicated time in a company-demarcated physical space allowed them quickly to absorb the company's culture in action, observing the acceptable behaviors that the corporate values defined. Cary felt new hires could accelerate building connections and confidence through their in-person interactions with other employees.

Using a "Hub and Club" concept, Cary and regional executives categorized key strategic office-based activities:

- Management Hub: for executives convening to discuss progress and issues

- Training Club: for new hires starting work and for general ongoing skills instruction

- Confidence Club: for all employees to gather and develop interpersonal relationships

It took Cary several months to assess and devise the strategy and tactics for the delicate equilibrium he wanted to achieve. Since some leases had to be decided upon and locked in by mid-2021, they rolled out home-office policies in each location and moved two offices, monitoring progress in anticipation of some fine-tuning over time. Cary feels that there is still a lot to learn about hybrid working that needs to be considered, as workflows will have to be adapted in order to maintain productivity and output levels.[2] Throughout the process, Cary demonstrated many key attributes of his empathetic leadership, recognizing, listening, accommodating, and supporting everyone across the division. He felt he was well equipped and prepared to usher his business through changing conditions with engaged managers and employees who were ready to adapt.

Mindset

But what is the right solution? What is the appropriate combination of work arrangements to optimize results at your organization—for the business and workforce? Whatever your objective, start with your attitude. Whatever model you are working with, whatever configurations you are working on, whatever policies you put together, workplace flexibility is a mindset first and policy second.

This point sounds simple, but it is profound. Without the mindset, no new working model is executed effectively, because it does not have fundamental buy-in. It will be all name and no substance if some executives or managers are not truly on board with providing genuinely flexible working options to workers. Workplace flexibility policies cannot satisfy workers' needs if employees do not feel comfortable taking advantage of the options offered. I have seen many programs fail, with low participation rates, because employees know, believe, or fear that relationships with their managers and their careers would be impacted negatively if they did participate. Executives may have touted such policies to attract talent, but this ruse was evident to employees who consequently did not sign up.

What is the mindset that you need to have? The mindset that Cary demonstrated: an open, inclusive, and empathetic mindset. You acknowledge and try to understand each employee in your company, department, or group as an individual with specific needs, preferences, working styles, and obligations. The ultimate objective is to enable each person to be engaged in their work and achieve the most effective setup for their working life, while also accommodating the needs of the business and any team members they work with. This essential mindset emphasizes equitable treatment across the workforce, so that everyone feels welcomed, valued, and supported, which also supports the achievement of the best outcomes in new work environments.

If the mindset is not fully there, restrictions may well be limiting and out of sync with cultural elements and values. Employees will undoubtedly recognize contradictions, and all the benefits of new working options will not be realized. In 2017, I was chatting with an inclusive, experienced CEO who focused on engaging employees, understanding how important that was to produce stellar results. However, I was surprised when our conversation touched on workplace flexibility.

"But our employees aren't that productive working from home," he told me. "They are allowed to work from home on Wednesdays, and it's their least productive day."

"I'm not sure I understand," I said. "You really understand how each person has different needs. Fixing the day seems inconsistent with your culture. Why only Wednesdays?"

"I noticed people are less productive because they take all their appointments on Wednesdays. I worry people's productivity would decrease if I expanded flexible work to other days. I also worry about losing our magic. We have a great community, and I don't want to lose that. We are going through a high-growth phase, and I am concerned about keeping our culture strong if people are working remotely on other days."

I empathized. I sensed his concern. I also recognized the self-fulfilling prophecy of workers scheduling all their appointments on Wednesdays, which was confirming the CEO's fears about reduced working hours that day. In fact, employees using Wednesdays for appointments was likely optimal for the company, too. People's doctors and dentists are often close to home, so employees would likely lose less working time going to their appointments from home rather than from the office.

The CEO also revealed to me, surprisingly, that his thoughtful leadership and focus on the employee experience had not yet dismantled his contradictory, subconscious bias towards office-based working. He was passionate and intentional about the company's future success—for everyone involved. However, his trust seemed undermined by stress about losing what he viewed as their competitive edge: their culture and community. His hidden fears had led to potentially unsettling cultural inconsistencies.

Does any concern or confusion strike a chord? Has the current flexible work model at your company not been as successful as you had hoped—yet? Are there employees who have to work on-site who have not been offered enough flexibility yet? Have you sensed any holdouts at your company inadvertently or deliberately causing subterfuge? Senior management may have very different philosophies and assumptions about the appropriate positioning and suitability of office-based working for themselves and their constituents, from zero to 100 percent of the time. Progressive and regressive employment models and configurations were primed to collide in 2021 as different employers and leaders responded with vastly divergent approaches.

Implementations are also complicated by executives' and employees' diverging ideas about the definition, appropriateness, and necessity of office-based safety measures. Every leader across your organization needs convincingly to accept full execution of any new configuration of work arrangements. Aligning assessments and rewards with example-setting and promoting utilization reaffirms a company's commitment to new configurations and encourages laggers to embrace the new model and recognize the benefits themselves. Every worker can then be comfortable taking advantage of whatever arrangement suits them (and the business) best.

Motivation

Aligned motivation and mindset lay the foundation for success. Why has your company *really* wanted to implement workplace flexibility? Is the reason primarily to achieve real estate savings? Is the main objective to hire more women, who have historically needed flexibility because of caregiving responsibilities? Or does your company want to attract and retain programming talent who many not be comfortable with social interaction and prefer to work in isolation? These motivations may be broad-based and genuine, but they are also likely to result in limited acceptance and success, without fully embracing an individual employee-focused, empathetic mindset.

Are flexible working options offered or positioned as motivation for employees? Are they earned or withdrawn, depending on employees' performance? Positioning new working choices as benefits is incongruent with the mindset that underpins effective flexible working and runs contrary to the reality that it is in the company's interest to roll out more flexible work models. Executives and managers wanting more engaged employees, improved performance, and reduced turnover provide more flexibility in order to improve the employee experience.

Employees' reasons for wanting a particular work arrangement are generally not relevant—whether working from home supports elder care or enjoying life in another city—since inclusive equitability is a founding tenet of successful implementation. However, some employers ask about the motives of employees for specific requests, which can lead to negative judgments about choices or relative situations. To mitigate differential treatment, asking reasons is best avoided.

In 2017, after I presented at a New York accounting firm, one senior partner told me, "I will do something I enjoy when I retire." He had a few years yet to go, and then he planned to become a college counselor. Trying to shake the legacy connection between work and suffering and emerge from the pandemic, millions of employees started rethinking their working lives in 2021 and resigning. Workers in the United States, where the social contract was most broken, were especially thoughtful about new options, having long endured an onerous work culture, arduous hours, and no job security.[3] Having more options, more control, and more intentionality about our working lives is long overdue, so that retirement is not the first time we can start enjoying what we do!

This significant mindset shift to empathize with employees' experiences, needs, and desires takes time. But I witness extraordinary outcomes that are mutually beneficial, since people contribute more when they enjoy more of their working lives and their leisure time and are less stressed managing their family obligations.

Mix

This feedback cycle is an integral part of the refining process to settle on the appropriate combination of flexible options for your company's particular workforce, including relevant choices for manual and knowledge workers and considering employees who must work on-site and those who are location agnostic. This mix encompasses freelancers and contractors as well, since their inclusion is important for accomplishing all the tasks and projects necessary to fulfill your business's needs.

Only corporations that launched fully remote from the beginning have avoided the significant challenge of thoughtfully framing and designing their hybrid work models. I imagine you have already gone through several iterations to make it work. It can be a rocky road to start with.

At the same time, new work models are not fixed, nor are they set for years at a time—that is the nature of the world, and marketplace, we live in now. There will be adaptations that are relevant, based on the following:

- New technologies: These might allow much more engaging video calls, encouraging even more remote working.

- New team members: People will undoubtedly desire a different combination of work arrangements, which, in turn, might require offering new options or different support.

- New business needs: These could warrant new selections, schedules, days, and timing based on expansion into new markets, new customer demands, and more.

- New workers: Contractors or a new or expanded group within your workforce might then affect employees' arrangements, in order to work most effectively together.

Plus, contingency plans, personal mini-crises, and other unexpected situations may effect change. In other words, flexibility provides give in the system for irregular incidents, both professional and personal.

Meaning

Innumerable misinterpretations and misunderstandings about non-traditional work models lead to talking at cross purposes. Resistance also arises if more extreme definitions are assumed, so clarifying the terms in any discussion is vital to ensure everyone uses terms in the same way. Here are key useful definitions:

- REMOTE WORK: Work is done outside the office any day, or days, of the week, at home or another location. "Fully" or "100 percent" remote means non-office-based work every day of a normal workweek. Remote working does not preclude client site work or off-sites. (Tax-related definitions differ.)

- HYBRID WORK: The workweek combines a mix of office-based and remote work, at home or another non-office "third" location, which typically offers functional workspace with a (much) reduced commute.

- VIRTUAL: Work is accomplished online; for instance, via video calls.

- FLEXIBILITY: Work models which focus on providing more autonomy and choices to employees. Arrangements may be set for long periods or be shorter-term and more fluid.

Other, less obvious, misinterpretations arise as a result of unclear communications. For example, stressing the importance of "being with" or "there for" clients often would *not* mean having a physical meeting—the client might prefer a video or phone call or even an email. However, for other circumstances an in-person discussion could be the most desirable option.

If you are clear and are deliberate about communicating details, you can uncover tacit assumptions and can review and discuss potential misconceptions. Decisions can then be based on what you are trying to achieve and optimally executed by employees to achieve objectives along the Customer Journey. Modes of execution and clients' preferences will evolve as more engaging technology solutions come online that provide more compelling and effective virtual experiences.

Model

The appropriate model for your company, division, or team depends on the needs of your business and workforce. If you are interested in optimizing your current model and possibly modifying options offered, as well as updating flexible work practices, it pays to revisit the foundational mindset and motivation first, since your model may have been launched a while ago.

Convene a group representing a diverse selection across the company to consider and achieve consensus about the degree of flexibility to be offered. What variety of options and range within those choices do executives, managers, and employees fundamentally believe provide appropriate flexibility for the business and workers? Then confirm: Are those options currently being offered? If not, what is missing? Or what alternatives were offered but not taken up? (Were they ineffectively communicated or was there some hidden resistance?)

Based on the culture and the mindset the organization embraces, the core premise of the operating model should resonate with everyone, and all options should be readily available for use by everyone, within reason. Some jobs may simply not allow for the location flexibility that others can incorporate; however, scheduling and other options provide important alternatives for these employees to ensure everyone has reasonable choice. It is important to uncover the causes of anomalies in the usage patterns, especially if particular choices were originally requested but never taken up.

Your company may have decided to impose certain limitations. That is a leadership choice and may be practical, in which case, it behooves managers to communicate the reasoning in order to eliminate any guesses or resentment about restrictions. For example, the Australian collaborative software development company Atlassian announced a flexible hybrid policy that allows employees to work anywhere remotely, so long as the company has an office in the country.[4] This type of restriction is very practical based on the unavoidable considerations of costs, regulations, taxes, and other legal requirements associated with employees' locations.

In my experience, formalizing workplace flexibility, particularly involving a diverse employee group, is always beneficial, especially to ensure sufficient resources are allocated to provide equitable support. Cultural incongruencies can also be surfaced and worked through. In addition, the same selection should be officially offered to every person in the company (with reasonable and communicated modifications based on job function parameters). Otherwise, all too often with informal flexible working environments, different divisions, teams, or people end up getting different degrees of flexibility. Discrepancies easily lead to resentment, reduced engagement, and other issues with the group perceived as being permitted the least favorable choices.

To evaluate how to optimize your company's flexible work model, it is beneficial to collect data on the current usage of existing options to see what employees have mostly, rarely, and never selected, and why. You can glean insights from operations' logistics feedback, such as information relating to time-tracking, tools usage, and document access, to assess where operational challenges exist and how those might best be rectified. Employees at all levels of the organization are also important sources of data, and many welcome sharing their experiences of hybrid and remote work situations and have possible suggestions for improvements.

Empathizing with employees in this review procedure does not mean that the company accommodates every new request. It is part of the process of understanding the realities of the current model in order to decide how to optimize it for the future. Flexibility means just that: there should be suitable capacity for special situations, without giving anyone inappropriately different working terms. Your corporate culture and values should allow you to determine what is "appropriate" in any particular case.

You can also discover the benefits of demonstrating heightened empathy practices along the way. The act of listening and an expressed intention to understand, manifested by asking questions to find out people's experiences, opinions, and recommendations, yields positive reactions. Indeed, follow-up and clear indication that actions were taken based on solicited comments is also a vital part of the process.

If some inputs were not incorporated, explanations allow employees to comprehend the process and conclusions. No action and no clarifications result in worse sentiments. Think about how you have felt when you were asked for your opinion, but then your views appeared to be ignored. Next time around, you were not engaged in the process—why bother?

Management

Give them an inch and they'll take a mile!

Do you believe that about your coworkers? Does anyone at your company? A hidden skeptical attitude or doubting undercurrent can be divisive and destructive for effective execution of any hybrid work model, especially as it casts negative aspersions on those not physically present.

I have heard this kind of mistrustful sentiment many times in the context of work. One CEO said it to me about the more than 30,000 employees at his company. He was predicting the outcome of giving all employees meaningful flexibility. I asked him, "What if employees didn't take a mile, but took an inch or two, but still got their work done—what then? With a focus on results, and if people still performed, what about them having an inch or two more?" He acknowledged this might be fine for some employee groups, but not all.

What do you believe about your team? How much do you trust them? What respect have you shown them, and how have they responded? How much are employees in your organization or unit evaluated based on outcomes? Have you given them objectives that they managed to accomplish?

What happens when someone blows their deadline or produces abnormally poor-quality work? Rather than berating and punishing the person, does someone question them empathetically to find out if anything is wrong and how to support them getting back on track? How have you been testing and refining the best configuration for each person's new work arrangement? How have you been checking what oversight would be optimal for each of your reports?

A results orientation is the most effective way to focus everyone on what needs to get done and—where resistance remains—draws attention away from where employees are physically, who can see them, what they are doing, and how. What matters is to achieve assigned tasks and goals satisfactorily within the time specified. In trusting environments with a focus on outcomes, employees—treated as adults—perform very differently than in fear-based conditions with micromanaging and intrusive monitoring, no matter where they are working.

Since hybrid models are also more complex to manage than entirely office-based arrangements, training for leaders, including all managers up and down the organization, is critical. Effective management obviously is not accomplished by walking around the office anymore or broadcasting one-way directives. Instead, the human-centric approach means tailoring oversight for each person, especially as individuals' different work styles appear more pronounced across their varied work settings.

Younger employees often benefit from guidance and clarity about process options and building blocks to organize their tasks and channel their energies, especially when testing more flexible work options. Then they can figure out "how" they prefer to accomplish their work. Older employees may be less comfortable with certain technologies or have well-established habits to modify, replace, or even "unlearn." Change-management resources can significantly improve lags in fully adopting effective new habits for distributed working.

Iteration is the name of the game to achieve a model that flexes to encompass everyone, along with a focus on results combined with clear metrics and measurements. Recognize and champion managers who encourage open discussion that assists distributed team members in accomplishing their tasks by prompting them to reach out if they need direction. Reward managers who exemplify empathetic behaviors and nurture employees' remote working skills by

- discovering what processes suit them;
- deepening relationships across the team;

- promoting collaboration through active listening and asking open questions;
- sharing accountability explicitly aligned with skills and strengths; and
- offering individualized support for achievement of the objectives set.

Managing remote workers easily becomes strained and ineffective with tight, centralized control. Instead, focus on updated practices that apportion responsibility, whether individuals or groups are solving problems or accomplishing tasks, no matter where they are working.

Mechanics

CULTURAL CORE. To support and successfully maintain a hybrid or remote model, a strong and cohesive corporate culture is a top priority. Your culture creates and nurtures the community that connects people traveling or working remotely, ensuring everyone feels a sense of belonging—that they are included and valued—driving engagement and fostering their full contributions. Values also influence actions, giving younger employees important guidance as they make decisions when working remotely.

APPROPRIATE ATTITUDES. Certain mindsets and practices are critical for generating a sustainable, connected, and engaging environment for coworkers who are not co-located: inclusiveness, transparency, and open-mindedness. These tenets drive executives' and employees' behaviors that mutually reinforce consistent, productive, and equitable virtual interactions.

DEAL BREAKERS. It is advisable to set, from the highest level, only a few umbrella terms that apply to every employee.

For example, the US bank Citigroup's main stipulation is that employees are in the office three days a week. Atlassian's key terms are convening at the office four times a year and working in a country where they have a corporate office. John Lewis Partnership in the United Kingdom reported they "won't tell our head office partners where to work."[5] Then, the devil is in the details—or execution—which is why your corporate culture and values matter.

FRAMING FLEXIBILITY. How do you make the hybrid model work for your business and each person? How has your company been configuring and managing everyone's different schedules? One person might have asked for only one day remote because of elder care needs, while another might prefer to work from home most days to handle school runs. What about those with long commutes or who want to live in a different city? What degree of flexibility is technically possible for each role? What has been accommodated so far for different schedules and configurations?

In the United Kingdom, a viable framework for workplace flexibility became law in 2014. Any employee who has worked at least twenty-six weeks at a company (although this period may be reduced significantly) has the "Right to Request Flexibility."[6] They can ask for any type of workplace flexibility so long as their desired work arrangement would not be detrimental to the company's business. The company has nine legally defined reasons for which they may deny the person their request, all related to a potential negative impact on business results. The onus is on the employee to decide what flexibility they need or want and to propose an arrangement—compromising with their manager and any team members—to achieve it. This approach is ingenious in accommodating innumerable different negotiated work arrangements that fulfill both compliance regulations and employees' desired situations. This UK law also offers a tried and tested end-to-end process for requests, corporate responses, negotiations, and implementation, if the framework your company has been using has been falling short.[7]

FIXED LOCATION. For the many employees who have to work part or all of the week on-site—at the office, factory, or other fixed location—focus on schedules, roles, and functions to give more autonomy and work flexibility. When Ricardo Semler became CEO of the Semco Group in Brazil in the 1980s, the company manufactured items such as pumps, dishwashers, and biscuit-making machinery. Ricardo gave production workers the ability to set their own (reasonable) production quota, work schedules, and intra-team job functions. They formed "manufacturing cells" sharing job functions, taking responsibility for quality, and working weekends when necessary. High productivity and low turnover were testament to this approach.[8] Operational situations offer different possibilities, so survey on-site employees, who are most familiar with their roles and tasks, to suggest what flexibility would make a difference. They are certain to propose some innovative ideas.

CLEARING COMPLIANCE. Different countries, states, provinces, and even cities have wide-ranging terms in their employment and tax laws. The UK model was also adopted in Vermont and the city of San Francisco around 2014, with some edits. So there are highly flexible frameworks your company could review and borrow from.

Employment jurisdictions can create administrative legal headaches, which is why Atlassian's framework allows employees to work only in countries where they have an operational base. Check regulations carefully when adding

permissible work locations to ensure compliance requirements are understood and viable (within reason). Practical
constraints still allow a wide variety of options and configurations for employees, and regulations are being updated
frequently with improvements.

RESULTS FOCUS. Another foundational shift is to focus
on outcomes that practically enforce the commitment to
performance over presence. Employees have varying times,
spaces, and solo/group environments that stimulate their
particular peak flow. They also prefer specific applications
or media. Individual preferences often become more evident
when working in isolation or away from the office. Managers practicing empathy, who adjust for personal differences,
are rewarded with improved performance. When focused
on results, with flexible options and customized oversight,
employees can optimize their work conditions and flow,
which can also be important for keeping everyone convinced
of the benefits of workplace flexibility.

UNIT COMPROMISES. Your company may be doing well
dealing with all the different arrangements that employees
want by organizing and managing them at the unit level.
Core mechanics rely on configurations that are discussed
and agreed among the leader and members of that unit, such
that preferences may be discussed and empathetic compromises made to arrive at the best overall solution and ensure
business results are achievable. With limited umbrella terms,
negotiating at the unit level allows for different team composition, changing circumstances, and inevitable contingencies.
Employees working on multiple projects complicate the
combinations and scheduling, but sophisticated software
supports proactive adjustments so team members can work
together on a mutually beneficial basis.

COMPONENTIZING WORK. For projects staffed with distributed teams, every element needs to be clearly defined, with tasks and responsibilities distinctly assigned by project leaders and workflow updated deliberately for the geographic diversity. A critical piece is understanding where cross-dependencies line up, as well as adjusting team participants for similar time zones, where possible. Identification, understanding, and digitized recording of all workflow arrangements are critical, considering new business conditions. Your operations are then able to adapt to changes in customer behavior, vendor capacity and availability, and other local or regional circumstances.

ADAPTING INNOVATION. Non-co-located teams can choose from a range of digitally enhanced synchronous and asynchronous methods to devise relevant new processes. When Sacha Connor of Virtual Work Insider first went fully remote in 2010 while leading an innovation team at the Clorox Company, she could only view new prototypes via video call when one of her team members carried a laptop down to the basement of the Clorox headquarters, where the prototypes were. She and the team used a variety of (improving) technologies to devise new processes for experiencing prototypes in development and shifting from yellow sticky notes to virtual brainstorming software.[9]

The innovation process for Jeroen de Kempenaer, Lead of the Innovation Portfolio Management Practice at Philips Engineering Solutions, had many initial stages spanning multiple office locations prior to 2020. When the typically in-person project kick-offs went virtual, effective brainstorming was facilitated by multiple pre-meeting one-on-ones to gather ideas that could later be shared anonymously and safely—for introverts or those cautious about any suggestion's negative reception—with the full group. Jeroen believes that just 5 percent of innovation is about creativity, that there is no shortage of ideas, and that the process of getting ideas realized is the key.[10]

ENABLING TOOLS. In a digitized and distributed new era of work, technology plays a strategic role, permitting seamless connectivity to bridge employees' work locations. Viewing your IT group as a productivity center rather than a cost center is a valuable strategic adjustment. Laurel Farrer, CEO of Distribute, a consulting firm specializing exclusively in remote work and virtual organizational development, emphasizes your organization's "tools are now your employee experience" since they host the majority of team members' time, output, and interactions. She stresses that your HR and IT groups need to work together to integrate the human element and create an effective "virtual employee experience" which the tools help fulfill.[11]

In addition to easy communication and project management capabilities, what tool functionalities do your teams need? After observing much uncoordinated purchasing of tools during 2020 and 2021, Laurel stresses governance systems, which inform how tools are used, integrated, and navigated between to facilitate effective workflow. "Effective virtual collaboration isn't dependent on purchasing the latest and greatest technology," she advises. "How you use your tools is more important than which tools you use." Successfully governed and balanced toolkits should not only facilitate efficient communication and workflows, but also measure worker wellness and strengthen company culture.

CRITICAL CHITCHAT. Relationships are important to nurture across a distributed workforce to keep building trust and find more common ground and points of connection, which all improve employees' empathy for each other. At HubSpot, the team of Brian Bresee, Director of Sales for the North American Partner Program, was already almost entirely distributed before the pandemic. They had discovered the enduring value of regular "remote water cooler" video chats to share experiences and ideas and to catch up personally. They supplemented these with monthly online and in-person events, such as Remote Trivia and Mystery Dinners.[12]

Empathetic understanding and relationships generate the most productive interactions, which are especially important for distributed employees. Strong bonds at Fuze, an enterprise-focused cloud communications provider, are purposefully stimulated to facilitate easy exchanges and information flow. The company promotes a lively, integrated social side in multiple ways, including numerous events, large messaging capabilities, and non-work-related group chats.[13] Their open approach generates incoming employee contributions: to give employees a voice and vote, their inputs are regularly solicited and incorporated. Employees offer valuable suggestions for improvements and updates.

HEURISTIC HIRING. During recruiting conversations, empathetic discussion of your organization's work options and practices can ascertain mutual fit. Sharing details with candidates about how your model works, what is involved, and previous positive and negative reactions reveals comfort levels and relevant onboarding needs. Some employees and new hires struggle to adapt their work routines, but mindsets and behaviors can always be learned with suitable support.

INFORMATIONAL ITERATIONS. Not only is your new combination of work arrangements likely significantly more complex than your previous traditional setup, but it is also just one piece of your business's necessary transformation. Any initial plans are provisional, and numerous trials and tweaks help you achieve a viable sustainable model. Regular reviewed iterations help you adapt to ongoing changes with a dynamic talent pool who look for different experiences.

Monitoring and Metrics

A well-structured performance management system that has detailed, agreed objectives and regular check-ins to monitor progress and adjust for new conditions is key to transitioning to hybrid and fully remote work arrangements effectively. Sacha Connor believes her successful move to fully remote working at the Clorox Company in 2010 was crucially supported by clearly defined projects with trackable measurements.[14] Senior management could have comfort that she was on track, while she understood what she had to achieve and how success was being evaluated.

Feedback from team members informs iterative improvements. Sacha made a habit of (anonymous) surveys to check in on any remote teams she leads to ensure they feel connected and that trust-based relationships that allow effective distributed collaboration are building.[15] Other metrics to survey include quantitative and qualitative data:

- Percentage of uptake of different options to check participants' comfort levels and hidden obstacles

- Employee sentiment, especially relating to remote workers' feelings of inclusion and support

- Comfort with and use of technology platforms

- Accessibility to senior management and career-development prospects

- Exit reasons in case the work arrangement has been a factor in a departure decision

Using software to track keystrokes or physical presence and eye movements seems oppressively controlling. Such technical solutions to check employee compliance expose a deeply unempathetic lack of trust and respect for workers that can only discourage engagement and hurt productivity. In any case, ingenious ways have been found to trick the software—not the desired result or optimal use of employees' efforts. Meanwhile, less intrusive means—such as frequent milestones—can be appropriate if fitting an individual's optimal work style, discoverable through empathetic exploration of their experience.

Momentum

What new work habits have your distributed employees and teams developed so far? Effective remote working and collaboration habits are not self-evident and generally differ substantially from what works in-office. Enabling and maintaining a new model requires establishing new habits that highlight and promote

- relationship-building and community;
- open, flexible, and inclusive mindsets;
- active and equitable communication;
- seamless (video-rich) interconnection;
- sharing of insights and data; and
- defined, componentized, and clearly assigned digital workflow.

All these dimensions are supported by clear accountability, defined expectations, and appropriate training. The COVID-19 pandemic created a petri dish of experimentation and discovery you are benefiting from as you establish new work practices. You are defining, clarifying, and testing particular approaches and actions to adapt and to repeat purposefully and consistently.

All members of a distributed workforce are dealing with different work circumstances, whether they are predominantly in the office or elsewhere. Adjusting management methods and operational practices is essential to achieve and maximize productive collaboration, starting with nurturing a cohesive community and meaningful connections among all your workers. Good technical connectivity and tools that cater to individual work styles and needs are critical. Above all, new management and operating practices require thoughtful guidance and support to enable a successful transformation.

Must Have

As a leader, it is understandable to want to feel in command again, to recapture a sense of control. That is how we were working for decades. I get it. When employees are out of sight and widely dispersed, it can feel too amorphous and chaotic. The company can feel as though physically prone and exposed. Achieving stability and security can naturally mean forming a close huddle.

Others may still have a strong desire for renewed physical orderliness. Perhaps you sometimes want to get back on track in a much lower-effort mode of operating that you could get your arms around—or feel that way, at least. Indeed, with such a harrowing extended crisis, we *all* want to reduce stress levels, expend less mental energy, be more comfortable, and feel supported by our (work) community.

The messiness of transition is as inevitable as the transformation itself. The new digitized business era requires new work models and approaches. Benefit from the elevated kinetic—and frenetic—energy to lean into the changes, continue to build momentum, and push through to implement your new work model fully and successfully. At the same time, your priority is to channel efforts to create, engage, and establish the new, flexible framework that your blended workforce needs, which means launching or reinforcing the empathy habits that support and sustain it.

Each chapter in Part III ends with habits to take away and practice so you can infuse your working life with empathy and reap the significant benefits described, always iterating through the THINK, FEEL, and ACT steps. Flip back to Chapter 6 and review the Seven Steps to Success to make the process as easy as possible and so you can guide others around you. Here is a quick recap:

1   PRACTICE: Use empathy as much as you can with a specific focus on developing two to three habits at a time.

2   PRIORITIZE: Apply empathy where you need to improve interpersonal dynamics the most first.

3   PAIR: Connect each new habit with a relevant part of an existing routine to make it easier to start and sustain.

4   PARTNER: Enlist someone for mutual support, increasing chances of success for each habit.

5   PLAN: Use a checklist to track your achievements and motivate continued practice.

6   PATIENCE: Give yourself the necessary breaks as you establish and practice new habits.

7   PROGRESS: Realize that it may be slow at the start but will accelerate, as each new habit has compounding effects and benefits and becomes much easier.

For more support, as I know this is not easy, I have provided a master list of empathy habits to easily pick from and prioritize at empathyworks.online, which has more details, tips, and support. Here are the first habits for you to review and choose from.

Empathy Habits

1 **Mind your mindset:** To facilitate the transition to new work arrangements, actively connect with people's needs and preferences and regularly remind yourself that the goal is to achieve mutual flexibility and responsiveness.

2 **Iterate often:** Start trials with clear timing and parameters. At appropriate intervals, gather qualitative and quantitative data to explore people's experiences, then use the data to refine, improve, and iterate again.

3 **Unlearn incompatible routines:** Take care that you and others do not slip back into any office-based habits that are not supportive of new work models. Help each other devise deliberate changes to previous activity sequences to help maintain new routines.

4 **Facilitate collaboration:** Establish facilitator roles for virtual team meeting protocols, designating or training participants.

5 **Emphasize location independence:** Practice inclusive virtual work protocols that combine remote and office-based workers so everyone participates equitably (e.g., all use video chat).

6 **Observe signals:** Proactively engage your empathy skills to notice body language, voice tone, email delays, and more, to assess the state of mind of non-co-located coworkers.

7 **Focus on results:** Modify evaluations to track outcomes and deliverables, shifting emphasis from presence to performance.

8 **Over-communicate:** The new rule is to share more, not less, when working across multiple locations. If in doubt, over-communicate to ensure everyone has the information they need and feels included.

9 **Clarify expectations:** Clearly define project objectives, tasks, requirements, and deliverables to promote mutually satisfactory accomplishments.

10

Culture
Nurturing the Foundation

W HAT ARE your cultural norms? Do you find shredded cuttlefish, snack bags of crickets, or cupcakes in the neighborhood grocery store you frequent? Are you likely to eat colored cereal shapes, meat floss, or cold cuts for breakfast? Do local buses run exactly on time, follow a general schedule, or happen along with luck? Would you wear red, white, or black to mourn someone who passed away? What parts of people's bodies do you find are acceptably bared in public?

The culture we live in has significant influence over us—every day, at milestone moments, and over our lifetimes. An expert on culture and branding, Jey Van-Sharp, Principal of MyÜberLife Consulting Group, who builds and advises companies at the intersection of culture, community, and commerce, defines culture as "the memories, the value system, the beliefs, the shared goals, the fears, the ideology, the mythology, that all exist within a community of people. Culture is the value system, the symbols, the signifiers, the lexicon, the apparatus that we exist in. Culture is the micro-cosm of how we interpret the world we exist in."[1]

Your corporate culture blends your company's vision, mis-sion, and purpose of commitments outwardly to the world and inwardly to workers. It is the fabric of your company, encompassing interwoven elements of vision and values. Cul-ture clarifies what matters and *how much* those things matter. Culture crafts the manifestation of your business and the means by which customers experience it. Cultural elements impact how much each employee focuses, applies themself, feels connected across locations, communicates effectively with others, and behaves in ways that are aligned and posi-tively reinforcing.

Molly Kellogg said that when she took over as CEO of Hubbard-Hall, "culture was the first thing I focused on. I made my ninety-day list and it wasn't finance, it wasn't sales, it was all about culture and resetting it because we had built up walls, we had built up jealousies and politics. So it was all about blowing that away."[2]

Corporate culture holds similar sway over us in our work situations as the connective tissue across working environ-ments at the office or creating microcosms for employees wherever they are. The culture creates the organizational space—physical and virtual—defining and setting the bound-aries of the intangibles of your organization's why, who, and how.

Think about a recent choice you had to make on a proj-ect or in a sales negotiation while working remotely or on a business trip. Do you recall considering what your boss or colleague would likely advise you to do? Did you think what the "appropriate" way forwards would be, checking previ-ous actions and decisions you and others made in the past? These behavioral nudges are determined—or at least greatly affected—by the corporate culture, particularly if the culture is articulated, cohesive, and actively manifested by leadership.

Mikael Sorensen explained that Handelsbanken "has always focused on a set of human values and believes in human nature, trusting people, and empowering them to take their own decisions."[3] Handelsbanken's culture and approach is lived daily, supported by its succinct "Our Way" booklet, which every employee has close at hand. Mikael describes "Our Way" as capturing Handelsbanken's "fundamental values and why we have those values, which benefit not only the customers and the staff, but all stakeholders."

The Business of Meaning

Many companies have a mission and a vision of what they want to achieve, which set the tone for the cultural environment. We are visually and viscerally aware of some of the most powerful ones in the public realm:

- Apple's trail-blazing push for us to "Think Different" has evolved into a mission to create the best user experience, improve the lives of people, and empower the public.

- Elon Musk's brash inspiration comes through in Tesla's chatty but serious employee handbook, which in 2020 stated, "We're changing the world. We're willing to rethink everything."[4]

- Richard Branson, Founder of the Virgin Group, blogs about Virgin's specific "culture of adventure" and that they "dismiss business as usual."[5]

These externally shared purposeful messages are all-important now as consumers—especially younger ones—look for meaning, ethical behavior, and sustainable operating principles from the companies they buy from. My Gen Z daughter researches and wants to buy sustainable products whenever possible. Jey Van-Sharp pointed out, "There are a hundred companies that make blue jeans. Which company are you going to buy blue jeans from? From the ones that care about the environment or the ones that are denying the environment? Are you going to buy blue jeans from the ones that are supporting racism or the ones that support equality?"[6]

Potential buyers and loyal customers also want assurance that the company is not guilty of social media's renowned superficiality and is attentively upholding and advancing its mission in sustainable, suitable ways—outside *and* in. Jey explained, "If your company, your employees, and the customers you serve are not aligned in cultural values, you will not have goodwill in the market. Branding is a point of view. People don't consume utility, they consume a point of view."[7]

Employees are also increasingly disturbed by outwardly lauded objectives that are not congruent with the internal corporate environment and treatment of talent. There must be consistency in culture and values across the business. A corporate purpose is extremely beneficial internally as well as for the business strategically. An elevated goal aligns and reminds every employee why they are there, giving meaning to their daily toil. When this high-level objective is clearly articulated and senior leaders frequently refer to it and connect projects to it, the leaders are empathizing with employees and satisfying a fundamental human need. People want to feel their work matters. They want to contribute to something bigger than themselves. Even on bad days, purpose can undermine that niggling feeling that no one cares... and "Why bother?"

Engaging employees is also an important benefit. Employees overtly recognize or intuitively feel when they work for an organization where they are heard and respected, and

believe that their contributions are valued and make a difference. Such a culture has an engaging and energizing effect.
People are prompted to apply themselves beyond the strict
scope of handling their daily tasks. Focused on a mission they
have bought into, workers are encouraged to put in that extra
effort and are more inclined to chat about a lingering work
problem while having a drink with a colleague at the end of
the day, mull it over on the way home, or reflect upon it in
the shower. Bingo! A new idea buds, a concept is advanced, or
a solution emerges. Multiply that across teams to see innovation efforts blossom and barriers to progress dissolve.

How is your company's purpose and culture expressed
and received externally? Does your company have a defined
purpose and articulated culture? Are these communicated
clearly in the marketplace? How does that affect the interest
of buyers and support conversions?

EXERCISE 1: Considering how customers view your offerings,
what could be communicated differently or what messaging
could be refined so they can better understand the important
cultural values?

What about internally? Contemplate your answers to the
following questions: Are people aware of how their efforts
contribute to fulfilling the overall mission? Do you personally
draw meaning from your work? How aware are employees of your company's culture and values on a daily basis?
Do your coworkers feel the same way? How do these emotions spur—or undermine—people's efforts?

EXERCISE 2: Find out how a peer of yours and a direct
report interpret and experience the corporate vision and culture. How different and aligned are their descriptions?

Scottish businessman Paul Reid is a serial entrepreneur. When he founded Sigma Seven, a mobile map-based solutions provider in the utilities sector, in 2000, based on his learnings and insights from his early employee experiences, he emphasized fostering a strong, connective culture.[8] The culture combined the vision and mission he had for the business and was purposefully based on core values of trust, openness, and transparency manifested by actively listening to employees and, most importantly, making changes based on their inputs.

Each person was there to challenge each other, do their best work, and contribute to improving the work environment and business results. Paul described the workforce of mostly software engineers as a family. Turnover was very low. He believes a significant reason for the successful growth of the company derived from the cohesive and trusting culture he nurtured. Employees worked closely together, having lively debates that generated innovative solutions. They were nimble and adaptive and often won business competing against much larger companies.

When Paul sold the company in 2015, it was subsumed into a company with tens of thousands of employees. The acquiring organization had decades-old protocols for communicating, data sharing, and responding to employee surveys. It did not take long for the different culture to affect employees and their behaviors. Absorbing new norms altered people's expectations, what they thought they should say, and how they felt they should act during meetings.

Similarly, culture influences actions as employees make judgment calls. This has heightened significance for a decentralized workforce. Culture plays an important role in creating the essential foundation of trust between managers and team members determining appropriate business choices from the range of available options. How is key data about context being conveyed to support decision-making as more autonomy is yielded to your distributed teams?

Attributes of Alignment

Another critical aspect is having a common target that everyone is focused on. Conflicting agendas can cause significant disruption to harmonious operations and effective achievement of work product, from small tasks to large projects. Therefore, highlighting and reiterating how siloed and cross-organizational efforts all align towards shared high-level goals supplants wasteful, divergent efforts and internal friction with channeled energies that compound.

Certainly, there is likely many more than one way to interpret your company's vision, leading to a variety of colleagues' opinions about how best to achieve it. Embracing a diversity of perspectives plays an important part in generating a rich range of possibilities to consider. Is the purpose of your business consistently understood? Do your colleagues have the same sense of what the business is trying to accomplish? Have you noticed any divergence among coworkers about where the company is going?

Scott Farquhar and Mike Cannon-Brookes, Co-founders of software developer Atlassian, have a clear vision for "unleashing the potential in every team" with an accompanying cultural value of openness to share and test ideas horizontally across the company.[9] This radical transparency and respectful dissent can lead to vibrant discussions about possible pathways forwards. They talk internally about "argue like you're right and listen like you're wrong," which does not mean everyone agrees or everyone's opinion is equal. However, they are open to new ideas, listening, and being wrong. They are also comfortable disagreeing and committing to moving forwards. A constantly evolving feedback loop allows refinement based on inputs from experts, customers, beliefs, and values, not ego.

With divergent destinations, such an open approach could fragment the workforce into camps competing against each other. It would be much harder to connect and empathize with colleagues' perspectives and ideas if people were going in different directions. Atlassian's senior executives are aligned in their mission and values and all sing from the same song sheet—literally dressing up in Elvis costumes and performing songs together on stage at their Summit in 2019—to rally everyone's shared inspiring objectives.

Integrated cultural elements need to drive all activities, big and small, overt and obvious, infused and implicit. Therefore, articulating your organization's vision, mission, purpose, and cultural values in writing, using language that is unequivocal, is very important. Indeed, capturing and recording these elements is crucial for fostering a sense of belonging and community for a company with remote workers or multiple offices or branches, just as Handelsbanken has. Your results from Exercise 2 may have already illustrated what aspects have not been described, understood, or experienced.

EXERCISE 3: Discuss with your peer and report how they and others might feel more connected to the mission and culture and what the resulting impact might be. In addition, solicit views from a diverse range of employees about your company's core values. Ask them each to choose five words that capture their sentiment about the essence of the organization and what it stands for. Combine, prioritize, and then test sample groups of five words across the workforce to see how they resonate. Do they inspire progress? Can they be communicated and repeated easily? Your company is unique in what words and values are relevant, actively manifested, and impactful.

The idea is to capture the spirit of the culture that exists, as well as highlight, or have a chance to elevate, particular values—like empathy. Whatever role you are in, you can also make a strategic difference as the division leader or team manager by integrating empathy as a value just for your group as a first step. The local effect will certainly infiltrate other areas and share the benefits further.

Culture Fit

Let's clear up a potential point of contention by clarifying definitions carefully. Having a cohesive culture is *not* about harmonizing personality traits, appearance, and characteristics. Strengthening your corporate culture is *not* about hiring people who have many of the same backgrounds, educations, hobbies, outlooks, or demeanors. Therefore, "culture fit" should not be interpreted as being about similarity that might limit diversity. Culture fit, the way I think about it, is about *alignment of values*.

Research by Lauren Rivera discusses situations where "culture fit" meant "cultural matching" and a "shared culture—particularly in the form of lifestyle markers," leading to inequalities and a lack of diversity.[10] With these definitions, her conclusion makes sense. Promoting inclusiveness and recruiting for diversity, not similarity, is essential for your organization. Let us recognize that the intention of "culture fit" as I define it is to align a diverse workforce.

Consider countries that have strong national cultural characteristics that also encompass broad varieties of people, personalities, and backgrounds. Cultural elements and values do not have to be homogeneous or indicative of similar properties, views, or experiences. In the same way, a company that has a culture based on timeless, unchanging values can embrace the broadest variety of employees. Your workforce can have strongly aligned values while also exhibiting a great variety of context, history, perspectives, and other critical dimensions of diversity. Which is why culture is the key—perhaps the only—way to create a strong, nurturing foundation that creates a welcoming environment for whoever supports the company's vision and values.

Enduring Values

Whatever your organization focuses on, especially during periods of transition and growth, which emphasize the need for a learning or student mindset, ageless values can provide meaningful support for your corporate community— understood, unchanging, and enduring. Whatever else your company prioritizes in addition to empathy, I believe several other values are important to integrate, since they are interrelated. In a business context, these are the following:

- TRUST: A connection built on mutually experienced reliability and commitment
- OPEN-MINDEDNESS: Willingness to consider other people's ideas and opinions that are new to you and different from your own
- INCLUSIVENESS: The ability to embrace many different types of people and treat them all fairly and equitably so they feel welcome
- FLEXIBILITY: The ability to change and compromise
- TRANSPARENCY: Open and honest communication, where information flows freely

- INTEGRITY: Firm adherence to a code of values, especially morals; a state of being undivided

And "safety." I was taken aback when I asked my daughter, a Gen Z in high school in 2021, what she would look for when she joined the workforce in a few years. Her first response was a "safe" environment. However, she was not thinking about "belonging" or "community"; she meant a workplace free of sexual harassment. She is certainly not the only Generation Z with this concern as a priority.

Finding the right values to highlight for any specific group of workers is key, and any divergent actors may part ways with your company—and executives and managers can expect that some people may leave (as Kimmi Wernli found, in Chapter 7). None of these values sits on its own. The consistency and coherence of our values and mindset is required so as not to raise concerns within our ecosystem.

When these values are interwoven, they create an unwavering and enduring cultural fabric and a corporate environment that

- welcomes every employee and treats them equitably;
- builds trust to cultivate a feeling of belonging;
- shares information widely to reinforce inclusion; and
- is adaptive and responsive.

With a cohesive set of values that includes empathy, employees are primed to communicate openly and clearly without fear of retribution, collaborate well and take risks within safe spaces where they feel they belong, and bring human-centric perspectives that are tuned in to customers' needs as well as colleagues' experiences. "You really cannot have a constructive culture if you don't have diversity, inclusiveness, and equity authentically embedded in your culture," explained Karyn Twaronite, professional services firm EY's Global Diversity, Equity, and Inclusiveness Officer.[11]

The Value of Trust

Indeed, trust and empathy are the most important aspects of your corporate foundation to focus on specifically. Trust also has a multidimensional effect, as Paul J. Zak's research on the "Neuroscience of Trust" showed. Employees in high-trust organizations are more productive and collaborate better with their colleagues. They are also happier with their lives and less plagued by chronic stress.[12] His work confirms that trust directly impacts people's ability to empathize, as it affects internal relationships. In high-trust companies, 11 percent of workers showed more empathy for their colleagues and were 41 percent less likely to depersonalize them than at low-trust companies.

Serial entrepreneur Paul Reid's third startup, Trickle, which helps organizations optimize employee experience, was launched in 2018 and finally formalized and encoded into software his methods of developing strong cultures with high employee engagement. His approach focused on developing trust, quickly, through an ingenious combination of anonymity and action, supported by transparency. It all started with his own experiences straight out of university working at a software startup that a lecturer had recommended. It was a good job, but working out of the co-founders' home, the environment was unstructured, ill-equipped, and not supportive of young, inexperienced employees, who soon started to grumble. After a year, Paul had opportunities to talk to other companies and was on his way out, but he wanted to do something.[13]

"Right, I'm going to leave," he said. "It's a shame that there are all these issues that people aren't talking about. Well, what have I got to lose?"

He decided to ask everyone which top two or three things bothered them most. He listed, categorized, prioritized, and anonymized their answers and saved the document as "Company-Issues.doc" on a floppy disk. Then, with butterflies in his stomach, he wrote his name on the disk and slipped it onto the CEO's desk when she was not there one day.

The next day, he got a call.

"Can you come out for lunch today with us?" The CEO asked him to meet with her, her co-founding husband, and another company director.

"Yeah, yeah, absolutely," he said. But inside he was thinking, *Ooh—what have I done here?!*

The group went to an eccentric pub in the heart of Edinburgh that was famous for not letting people in for no rhyme or reason. But the group was admitted and sat down. It was a good sign, but Paul was still nervous.

"Thanks so much for giving us an insight into these problems," the CEO said, starting the conversation, and Paul was very pleasantly surprised. "We didn't really know that there were so many things going on. We had an indication that you guys were disgruntled, and we heard some moans. But we didn't realize the extent of it." The executive trio found it helpful to have every issue listed and ranked, supported with numbers behind each issue—but without any names.

"Look, can you help us fix this?" they asked at the end. "Can you go back to the team and say that we are committed to making this better?"

Paul told me, "I'm a fixer, so I ended up staying for almost two more years. The team responded really well to finding out the founders were listening and were going to do something about it. We created a culture that moved from 'you need to create an anonymous document' to 'we'll talk once a month about things that are really bugging people.' The spirit was 'talk openly. We're all here to help each other.' It took a while. But the key thing was the founders came to the monthly meetings and quick action followed, which was usually a collaborative solution."

Paul's new company, Trickle, focuses on the positive outcomes of nurturing strong cultures—employees who are thriving, engaged, productive, and loyal. For employees to engage, they must feel comfortable sharing their ideas *and* issues openly. If assured anonymity, employees speak up, and if their comments are acted upon promptly, a foundation of trust can build quickly. From his own experience, Paul empathized with employees' potential concerns, so Trickle gathers no identifying data if comments are shared anonymously. However, over time, they have found the use of anonymity decreases as trust builds and openness and transparency increase.

People working at high-trust companies enjoy their jobs 60 percent more than at low-trust companies and are 70 percent more aligned with their firm's purpose, as well as having 41 percent more sense of accomplishment, according to Paul Zak's research on trust. A focus on trust as a core value is essential as a foundation of your culture and for other values and beneficial outcomes. Building upon the positive foundation of trust, employees reported 74 percent less stress, 40 percent less burnout, and 29 percent more satisfaction with their lives.[14]

Many different personal characteristics feed into and foster a trust-based culture, from those of executives to managers and even non-employees working on projects as part of blended teams. Such qualities identified by Consuelo Wilkins in her research include being accessible, approachable, empathetic, honest, and respectful.[15]

Trust also affects retention, with one study revealing that at high-trust corporations, 50 percent more employees expressed loyalty to their organization and intended to stay for more than twelve months.[16] These numbers become all the more significant during unsettled times, when keeping workers who are engaged, collaborating, and productive is of paramount importance.

EXERCISE 4: Conduct a thorough review of the strength of the cultural experience throughout the Employee Journey— from initial messaging by recruiters and hiring through to leaving by resignation, retirement, or other circumstances. Just as culture affects corporate branding and positioning along the Customer Journey, so too are cultural values— including empathy—applicable all along the Employee Journey. You can assess where cultural aspects might need greater attention, visibility, and expression.

Critical Grounding

Culture might have mattered less in previous periods, which were more settled and when we were comfortable in our routines, working steadily in the same location in clearly defined, predictable conditions. Corporate environments were standardized, although, frankly, dehumanized. There was little warmth and less connection, and we escaped from work at the end of each shift and day and dreaded Mondays. Work also provided stability.

Now, times are turbulent, as we try to define and transition to new equilibria. Don't you feel sometimes like you are scrambling to keep up with marketplace changes while also proactively pushing yourself and your team to come up with new operating rules? We all want new guidelines that reduce the effort we need to expend each day. We want—we need—to feel grounded, comfortable, belonging to a community that anchors us and provides some sense of stability.

Work relationships are not just about superficial pleasantries anymore; they touch upon values, beliefs, and more, to embrace the breadth and depth of each person with whom we interact. Your corporate culture has become more relevant and essential, as the foundation layer, the fabric, of your company. Especially when we are not co-located geographically, well-described and demonstrated company-specific tenets govern the way people act and point towards the best decisions.

We innately absorb the atmosphere, energy, and values that define our environment, which provides guidance, coherence, and support during times of change and uncertainty. Based on current conditions, not only is a strong culture important, but empathy is essential to include in the set of cultural values your company upholds.

Empathy Habits

1 **Consistently build trust:** Every day, nurture people's sense of belonging, promote openness so everyone feels safe speaking up, and support reasonable (defined) risk-taking.

2 **Make it matter:** Regularly connect employees with your company's purpose and how their work contributes towards progress.

3 **Emphasize alignment:** At milestone and period intervals, confirm common group understanding of objectives and direction.

4 **Model values:** Find ways to manifest corporate tenets in your daily work to reaffirm the guiding and grounding influence of timeless values.

11

The Contemporary Worker
Individual and Included

"WE ARE living proof that there is no one-size-fits-all policy for people. For inclusion and diversity to work, we have to recognize how different we all are, and with those differences come different needs and different ways to thrive. We feel that Apple has both the responsibility to recognize these differences, as well as the capability to fully embrace them."[1] So reads an employees' letter asking Apple's leadership team to reconsider its return-to-office policy in June 2021.

Each one of us is an individual. Each one of us wants to be appreciated as a unique and whole human being. We also each want to be, and feel, included in our community at work, to have a sense of belonging and be comfortable enough to speak up, participate, and perform. Purposeful effort is essential to welcome and integrate people across our many diverse human dimensions—such as race, age, gender, sexuality, and ability—so that every individual feels fully and equitably included.

Empathy—understanding both others' perspectives and experiences—is essential for creating an inclusive work environment. Integrating empathy means ensuring there is openness to and acceptance of every employee's individuality. Creating an empathetic environment requires stepping up to provide what it takes to help people thrive—being able to distinguish, embrace, and cater to a range of requirements. Work environments that sustainably support high-performing teams embrace employees as individuals with an inclusive mindset, so every person can show up as their whole self and do their best work.

In their letter, Apple's employees wanted to be heard and recognized. Each one of them. They wanted to be identifiable as individuals with different points of view, needs and desires, obligations, and experiences, which they felt their employer was not acknowledging. Apple employees felt that leadership's perceived lack of empathy was translating into omissions relating to key principles of diversity and inclusion. This mattered enough that the employees specifically called out the perceived unempathetic treatment:

"Over the last year, we often felt not just unheard, but at times actively ignored. Messages like, 'We know many of you are eager to reconnect in person with your colleagues back in the office,' with no messaging acknowledging that there are directly contradictory feelings amongst us, feels dismissive and invalidating."

Listening actively to people—so that they are aware that their words are respected and valued—is a first, fundamental pillar of any productive relationship and interaction. We all, individually, want to matter—in our personal *and* our professional lives. One core omission of Apple's was not to recognize that everyone who worked for the organization was an individual with their own needs that they wanted some flexibility to accommodate.

Understanding Uniqueness

We have learned much while operating under pressure during crisis conditions. Although the pandemic hit us all hard in different ways, a sentiment of vulnerability felt the world over was infused with our intermingled confusion, grief, isolation, and overwhelm. These common feelings allowed us a rare period of connection—across countries and cultures—and the ability to empathize with each other through our raw discomfort, pain, and sorrow.

We all understood better than before what being an individual meant—in isolation, in different settings and situations, under different pressures. We recognized each other much more as integral beings—comprehending new details about each other's contexts, backgrounds, and states of mind as we saw into people's "other" lives, and they into ours. We became starkly more aware than before what being included meant—being connected, coming together virtually, supporting and comforting one another across our disparate locations.

Recall how your appreciation of different colleagues changed as you noticed the details of their home-office settings. What more did the pictures on the walls, the books on the shelves, or the clutter piled up tell you? How did your connection change when you heard their barking dog in the background? What shifted in your relationship as you saw them coping with children's tugs on the sleeve or off-camera tantrums? How did that additional knowledge about your coworkers improve your communication with them, once you had more specific context, once you were able to empathize with them better? Did you notice how each person appreciated acknowledgment of their struggles and achievements in a slightly different way?

The sentiments were not all positive. What concerns or discomfort did you have when you realized what chaotic, cramped, or otherwise difficult situations some people were dealing with? With a more integral understanding of your team members and colleagues, what did you find out about how you could support them?

In crisis, differences were exaggerated and exposed, and empathy became a critical skill for bridging the gaps and helping us all rally together. We hope the most extreme conditions are behind us now. However, we can call on some of these memories and sentiments when we need to remind ourselves how different others' circumstances still are and what disparate experiences we are each typically having.

We benefit from paying attention to what management, motivation, and recognition each person responds to best, including how they react under pressure and how everyone best works in tough conditions. The reality is that in our everyday lives, minor crises come and go all the time, and ongoing uncertainties are likely to throw a wrench in smooth-flowing operations at random intervals.

The Balance of Needs

Every human being has a deep-rooted, inherent, and essential need to be heard and valued independently—from day one. In fact, an imbalance—or any recurring lop-sided weighting—of the shifting equation between parent and child, as the child becomes less dependent, often significantly affects the child later in life. Disequilibria frequently cause people to continue patterns later as they, often unknowingly, attempt to redress the inequities.

A colleague who heavily emphasizes their own agenda, appearing selfish or even narcissistic, is possibly continuing behavioral habits that they developed as a child. Conversely, someone else may rarely voice their needs because no one ever took them into account when they were growing up. There is no criticism implied, no right or wrong. This information about learned patterns of behavior, about what unintentionally drives certain types of interactions, can prompt helping nudges to stimulate communications that are more productive for all involved.

We are all somewhere along this continuum of how we want or are used to being responded to depending on the topic, our needs, or our dynamic with someone we interact with. Therefore, it behooves every one of us to pay attention to whom we are dealing with and what recognition they have of the equilibrium of the discussion and even relationship dynamics.

Healthy relationships and conversations demonstrate an equitable balance of interactions between the parties involved— with a sharing of stories and no one dominating a pairing or group in terms of airtime, concern (getting other people's), or influence. Over 50 percent of the sentiment two people take away after a dialogue derives from how much back and forth there was in the conversation. Beth Porter, CEO and Co-founder of Riff Analytics, discovered this sensitivity to the balance of interaction while conducting extensive research in behavioral science using artificial intelligence at MIT.[2]

The revealing data drive the application Beth went on to launch at Riff Analytics, which uses AI-enabled tools to help teams collaborate in virtual meetings where, she says, "everybody has to be engaged, so we measure engagement in a variety of different ways, and then we give people real-time feedback on-screen while they're in the video meeting to show where the dominance of the conversation is."[3] The application helps them manage their participation and encourage discussion that is positive and productive for everyone. Beth explained that the Riff platform can also generate pulse surveys after meetings to check what each person's experience was, asking, "How did that meeting go? Did you feel like you had a chance to speak? Did that feel like a good use of your time?"[4] With thoughtfully practiced empathy, inequities from learned early patterns that may now be automatic can be rebalanced, which also means toning it down or speaking up more if you have been less inclined to do so.

Facing Race

George Floyd's murder on May 25, 2020, was a tragedy and a turning point. The protests that followed across the United States and around the world elevated sensitivity and active listening, to hear countless harrowing stories of racial injustice, discrimination, and microaggressions that so many Black and Brown people have been suffering for so long. Locked down at home, vulnerable and raw from shock and grief, millions of people who, until that time, had not understood or realized the extent of the horrors and mistreatment received and absorbed the anguish and pain.

Every person had their own reaction and action to take. Deeply entrenched in work on empathy, mine began with trying to put myself in the shoes of the people whose stories I was reading and learning about. Until that point, I had been deeply ignorant. I had a shocking awakening. I should have known and understood much more. I was complicit. I had not been empathizing with the points of view and daily experiences of a large percentage of the population around me, living in New York City and far beyond. With much more historical detail and context, I could begin to contemplate what others had been through. I learned more about the sickening and devastating cascade of events over centuries, and my realization amply reinforced my belief that empathizing is critically about taking action with the deeper understanding gained.

With much greater comprehension of the painful events of the past, I became intentional about what I could do to change the situation in the present and for the future. I increased the emphasis on inclusion in my empathy work and learned more about what actions could be meaningful. For my podcast, I sought out corporate leaders to discuss their advocacy of empathy in the workplace that tied into their active and visible efforts to enhance diversity and inclusion at their companies. I interviewed several specialists in the diversity and inclusion field to educate myself about how to support environments where people feel included.

From my podcast and other interviews in 2020 and 2021 with experts and proactive business leaders, in which we discussed diversity and inclusion, the protests, and the possibilities for change, three main themes emerged: the need to aim for the truth intentionally; empathy's significance and role; and actions we can all take, as well as initiatives underway or anticipated.

AIMING FOR THE TRUTH. Recognizing the reality of where we are is the first step to making meaningful changes:

- Jey Van-Sharp, as a culture expert, observed, "We have to operate in a new framework. It's no longer the guy who's making the racial joke or the microaggressive or passive-aggressive joke. That's not how the world works. Everyone has value."[5] Jey was unequivocal: "The aim is not for comfort. The aim is for understanding and for truth. If your company is focused on truth as a value, you'll be on the right side of history. Or, if you want to be in denial of that, it's going to be very rocky."[6] He added, "We have to look at ourselves as executives, as businesspeople, as corporations, as brands, as part of the narrative of equality and justice. We don't get to exist outside of those worlds and pretend that we're going to hide. The rhetoric is right there. The culture has already shifted—if you don't choose a side, you are choosing a side."

- Jennifer Brown, CEO of Jennifer Brown Consulting, a diversity and inclusion specialist, remarked, "Many communities didn't feel seen or heard in the workplace and were struggling with inequitable policies, practices, and procedures. Organizations just weren't awake."[7]

- Mark Read, CEO of WPP, a global marketing and advertising agency conglomerate, recognized, "We've done unconscious bias training; I think that helps to a point, but I think you have to go beyond that. We have to create an organization where fighting racism becomes everyone's task."[8]

EMPATHY'S ROLE. Inclusiveness is closely tied to empathy. Certainly, some empathize and manipulate people with malevolence. However, for most, connecting with someone mentally and emotionally increases understanding and brings people together:

- Siham Awada Jaafar, President and CEO of 3D Consulting & Communications, and a diversity and inclusion specialist who founded the Images & Perceptions Diversity Conference, said, "I really believe empathy is the platform to build everything on. You feel that you cannot just accept people but empathize with their situation or empathize with their issues and you can create that acceptance."[9] She explained, "You have your way of thinking, I appreciate it, I accept it. Doesn't mean that I have to live it, but I accept it and I appreciate the concept that's how you feel. And you're right to feel that way. You're not taking anything away from me by doing that."

- Norman de Greve, CMO of CVS Health, is a long-time advocate of empathy. Discussing the protests in 2020, he said, "I think the lack of empathy is what's created most of our problems. If you want people to reach their potential, you cannot operate in a way that doesn't encourage them to do that." He was frank: "What I think that we all have to realize is, whatever we've done, it hasn't been enough."[10]

- Mark Read sees empathy as critical going forwards. "If you don't have empathy or you don't try to understand where other people are coming from," he said, "I don't see how you understand their situation or the issues that they're facing. I think it's essential."[11]

- Jennifer Brown said, "Ideally we all move forward together with empathy for each other's journey, because there is not a single one of us that hasn't had an awakening."[12]

EMBRACING PROGRESS. We all can make a difference, every day, by launching and sustaining large and small initiatives focused on diversity and inclusion of every nature in our companies. We can choose to speak up and be allies when our empathetic connection helps us recognize when someone may feel excluded, unappreciated, or disrespected:

- Jey Van-Sharp's advice was to "have real, authentic conversations from a place of understanding. Don't try to speak on the behalf of people you don't understand, or groups of people, or genders you don't understand. Bring those people in, lend them your platform. Invest in them, train them, listen to them. View your company as a platform of empowerment."[13]

- Siham Awada Jaafar encouraged practicing empathy. "Get to know other people, get to know their backstory. Sometimes people react to things a little bit differently, and you need to know why. It's not taking it personally; it's understanding that backstory. So just be cognizant of the other person and what they're going through."[14]

- Norman de Greve explained, "We really have to step back and take a look at this. I don't think it's just about giving donations to places or press releases. I think it's about taking meaningful, tangible steps on the long journey forward to building trust, building inspiration and connectivity, and through empathy, so that people feel like they have the opportunities they deserve, and by doing that they bring all of their abilities to work every day."[15]

- Gena Cox, PhD, CEO and Founder of Feels Human, and an inclusion strategist and organizational psychologist, told me, "Focus on helping leaders figure out what are the biases built into standard practices and procedures that are perpetuating the problem."[16] Gena also said, "If you hire more people of color into an organization that does not support inclusion, you are going to end up with a lot more unhappy people, because you have to build a culture of inclusion to support them."[17]

- Jennifer Brown said, "It would make it easier if people revealed 'Hey, I'm an aspiring ally; I'm on this journey. Here's what I'm learning and here's where I'm going to utilize what I have to be in solidarity and to change outcomes for others.'"[18]

- Karyn Twaronite, EY's Global Diversity, Equity, and Inclusiveness Officer, urged, "Start measuring your own accountability. Check your baseline—see where you are and where you would like to go. Begin measuring your progress. If you do have a D&I [diversity and inclusion] leader, great. If you don't, identify somebody on the senior team to be a sponsor for this. Add it to the agenda for every one of your business meetings. D&I is a business topic."[19]

- Mark Read said, "We need to do more to be a company where people are comfortable bringing themselves to work. There are a number of the things we're doing—from allyship to understanding microaggressions and encouraging people to speak up, to having conversations about these topics."[20]

Active Inclusion

Inclusion, importantly, encompasses every aspect of diversity in addition to race—age, gender, sexuality, ability, and more. Whatever country you live and work in, whatever company employs you, your coworkers do not all look, sound, or act the same. Our different identities, personalities, cultural backgrounds, and other nuances make up the richness of who we each are.

Every company has employees who are diverse in multiple ways, and there is heightened awareness that many minority and vulnerable groups have borne the brunt of pandemic-related hardships, revealing as well as exacerbating discrepancies and discrimination. Racial and ethnic minority populations were disproportionately represented among essential workers and industries in the United States, bringing social and racial injustice and inequity to the forefront of public health, according to the CDC.[21] In Europe, vulnerable migrant communities were recognized as some of the people most negatively impacted by COVID-19.[22] In 2020, 54 million women worldwide lost their jobs, and, of those women, close to 90 percent left the labor force completely, compared with about 70 percent of men in the same situation.[23]

Even with strong economic rebounds coming out of the worst of the financial trough of 2020, reverberations from new variants and other lingering effects mean that general working populations remain sensitive to these inequities. Active inclusive adjustments are critical for reducing discrepancies. Moreover, with a corporate culture that encompasses empathy and other related values, overt attention to inclusion issues will continue to be important for every organization going forwards. We can recognize why when we consider current and future customers' and employees' experiences carefully.

Empathy augments your ability—with your consistent effort every day—to understand and welcome every employee's differences, both overt and subtle. When you show interest in them, as well as find points of connection, you enable the success of your team, department, and business. Adopting a deeply empathetic approach, you will be better equipped to strengthen your relationships, convert more sales, negotiate better partnerships, and cultivate high-performing teams.

More than anything you will be making mutually reinforcing, powerful human ties within your ecosystem, cultivating trust and strengthening bonds. Think of how much more productive *you* are when you feel accepted, welcomed, and comfortable. When each of your employees or team members feels truly included, they can do their best work.

There is nothing passive about what it takes to transform successfully in our evolving world. Proactive measures are required. We can act warm and friendly. That's great, but it's not sufficient. The more you step forwards, reach out, and make inclusive choices—especially embracing every individual employee for who they are—the more you can make decisions and take actions that give your company a competitive advantage.

Empathy Habits

1 **Embrace uniqueness:** Lean in daily to understand each person's specific context, background, and talents.

2 **Recognize needs:** Balance everyone's different situations and desires to create a supportive and inclusive environment.

3 **Promote diversity:** Proactively encourage efforts in all areas to expand and ensure the diversity of candidates and new hires who feel welcome.

4 **Identify preferences:** Pay regular attention to people's preferred working times and styles to assist your ability to adapt routines and compromise among teams most effectively.

5 **Support equitably:** Frequently affirm that every worker is getting the support and training they need to do their jobs well wherever they are working.

6 **Check assumptions:** Before responding, or taking any action, confirm you are sure you accurately understand the facts, the person's perspective, and their intentions.

12

Experiential Elements
Building Compelling Context

CREATING A competitive edge in attracting, hiring, and retaining the talent you need may be the most convincing argument that persuades you to focus on the Employee Journey. Let's acknowledge general compounding issues: the mismatch of education systems' output and enterprise needs; unrelenting technological progress requiring ongoing upskilling for most jobs; inattention and resistance from employees and employers to reskilling for increasingly digitally dependent roles; and growing long-term adoption of hybrid and fully remote models, meaning organizations around the world are competing for your talent now.

How many people in your organization are lifelong learners or somewhat open to learning new skills? How many positions do you currently have open that require a reasonable level of digital skills, and how many do you foresee needing over the next three years? Accelerated digitalization during the first waves of the pandemic further increased the need for technology skills and elevated the relative importance of your talent. Do you have a long-term skills-focused talent strategy yet? Of course, it is not just about workers having the necessary skills. You also need people engaged in their work when applying them.

For job seekers, the most attractive organizations focus on the employee experience, with

- a human-focused, trust-based, inclusive culture;
- a transparent and open approach with workers;
- an inclusive attitude to all employees' contributions;
- flexible work arrangements;
- comprehensive and customizable well-being programs; and
- support for employees' self-managed skills and careers.

Such companies are, in essence, empathetic and thinking about the perspectives, needs, and futures of their power base: their entire talent pool. The companies also recognize the symbiotic evolution of their business and talent, including how to develop employees in, around, through, and even back to their organizations.

Where are the gaps or areas along the Employee Journey that your company needs to update or augment? Let's explore key aspects so you can assess what changes will improve experiences for all potential, existing, and future employees and non-employees who contribute to your business' success.

The Engine of Growth

Who fuels your future? The perspectives and circumstances of your company's youngest cohorts are integral when setting the tone because of the relative breadth and depth of their digital education and early intuitive exploration of technologies. Their inputs and ideas are key. Meanwhile, just as many Millennials and Generation Zs, you have probably been paying attention to certain elements of the Employee Journey for a while, aware of different elements of the shifting work landscape. You may share many of their general cares and concerns about reduced financial security and uncertain future rewards and career trajectory.

What will entice Gen Z candidates to your team? What gives them confidence that they will be included and valued as employees, their opinions listened to and data shared with them? Can they be convinced that they will get the training they need to upskill and sustain the competitive edge of the business and themselves? If your senior executives are not focused on how to keep the newest recruits in an evolving market, who would join or linger long?

Paulette Rowe, CEO, Integrated and E-commerce Solutions, with the Paysafe Group, which is a leading global specialized payments platform, said, "It's not enough for people [Millennials] to be successful in the role, or feel that the company is doing well. They want to thrive and feel that they are getting personal growth, that we're investing in them."[1]

Employee Contracts

Whom did you last hire? For what reason and role? With what employment contract? Was that the optimal arrangement? The perfect candidate is not always going to become an employee. Your company needs the right complement of people and skills working to accomplish the business goals and advance towards its vision. Great candidates, especially for niche expertise, may often prefer not to become a full- or part-time employee, as working for multiple employers or clients can give them more financial stability, or their specific situation makes that a more desirable arrangement. Do you ever accommodate these options?

Perhaps your organization is philosophically or logistically still disinclined to hire contractors or only engages them for specific (non-strategic) tasks. Companies that resist the strategic investment of setting up non-employees to work effectively often find outcomes of outsourced tasks and projects are repeatedly suboptimal, so a self-perpetuating cycle exists. However, a surge of flexible arrangements offered to returning furloughed employees after initial COVID-19 lockdowns has changed some attitudes. In addition, specialized needs and increasing competition for specific skills are also influencing a changing stance.

What do you need to complete a project: easy access to direction, data, documentation, and any other necessary resources? Otherwise, you waste time and energy that could be spent optimizing results. Contractors also need to get hold of particular project resources using secure protocols applicable for non-employees.

New digital infrastructure has also automated portions of workers' tasks, which has often meant shifts in deployment and role. Implementing applications for pandemic-related remote working has also meant greater capacity to engage and support non-employees effectively. Going forwards, a variety of employment—including more non-employee—arrangements will be characteristic, catering to the flexible and financial needs of both your organization and the talent. Since millions of employees around the world are rethinking their working lives, it is beneficial for your company to be open to and participate in discussions about new arrangements and configurations.

Rethinking Recruiting

Where do you look for candidates? Is your company still limiting searches to the locale around your office(s)? Are you finding all the people your business needs? If not, then it might be an opportune moment for an important, *strategic* rethink.

If your company needs to expand the recruiting search radius, does that mean trying to persuade people—in other words, incentivize them—to relocate within an agreed "circle of comfort"? Or are you contemplating that some employees might now be fully remote? Such a move could require a substantial mindset shift for executives and policy changes for the existing workforce, to avoid creating a dysfunctional multiclass system. Or are you now thinking about hiring more contract workers who are generally remote in order to keep agreed location-based arrangements intact?

What is your company ready to tackle now and in the short- or medium-term? Hiring needs for growth may force your hand sooner rather than later. Therefore, now may be the time for thoughtful conversations about what employee arrangements are acceptable and supportable to transition to. Do not forget to discuss the associated updates necessary, such as optimizing for remote recruiting and onboarding, as well as enhanced connective community activities.

In recruiting efforts, underscore the benefits of empathetic interactions when interviewing candidates, as well as when considering existing employees for promotion. HubSpot emphasizes behavioral questioning to be able to figure out a potential hire's empathy skills and how well they will likely connect and work with customers and team members.[2] A bank sales lead deliberately seeks out individuals who are open-minded and curious as well as personable.

Paul Reid's company, Trickle, onboarded several new employees during the first year of the pandemic and did not meet them in person for months. Along with many other executives and HR professionals, Paul found onboarding remotely probably the hardest task to do well during the crisis, when it was not possible to assemble at the office.[3] However, virtual onboarding can be accomplished successfully with attention and design.

Beneficial activities include convening in person where possible, combined with frequent virtual gatherings, both formal and informal. Meetings involving people with a mix of roles and levels accelerates new hires' sense of integration, community, and confidence. Senior leaders can model company culture and values, reinforce the corporate purpose and objectives, and, most importantly, share motivating connection to future career opportunities. Surveying can help uncover aspects not covered sufficiently for your company, employees, and specific geographic spread, to create and strengthen beneficial connections.

In addition, launching a strategic overhaul of recruiting processes and practices to integrate relevant HR applications is valuable, considering new hiring mindsets, methods, and recent innovations. Attention to any embedded algorithms is important, to check for bias and current relevance, since they typically reflect status-quo thinking from the time they were initially developed. Many are not updated regularly to incorporate important new data and understanding, which can result in hidden disconnection or irrelevance during times of great change.

What Work?

If the point of work is no longer to put us on the pathway to heaven through suffering, is it not reasonable to shift our mindsets deliberately to maximize earthly outcomes for all involved?! Purpose can provide beneficial value to motivate employees and channel their concentration. How can you connect employees with what they are doing, what they care about and enjoy?

During his internship in summer 2021, my son, Liam, was greatly motivated by learning the "purpose of a menial task" he was working on. An executive asked, "Do you know why you are doing this?" and then, empathizing with him, sat down and gave him detailed context and concrete understanding of the fundamental layer his work contributed to the overall project. Liam and his work output benefited by his recognizing the broader context of the project as part of a strategic initiative.

When you strategically integrate empathetic assessments for employees, you can more easily discern what work content is most appropriate for each person so they can enjoy what they do, feel fulfilled, and perform as well as possible. Gallup research in 2019 shows that orienting employees towards their strengths and skills increases engagement, as well as boosts revenues by 10 to 19 percent and profits by 14 to 29 percent.[4]

The evolving technology landscape has widespread impact, shifting work focus to the skills needed to accomplish tasks rather than a specific job title. Some companies find it more sensible to craft roles for each worker based on their specific skills. After matching people and current tasks as far as possible, gaps are then filled in by other employees, part-time positions, and contracted resources, depending on the type and timing of the tasks involved.

How to Work

Work used to be simple, slow, and steady. We could be told what specific, repeatable steps we had to take. A former investment banker told me a key daily task of his first job at a major commodity trading firm in the late 1980s was simply to input into a large mainframe computer specific data that needed reconciling at the end of the day. We also had years to learn our jobs, watching over and being watched by more experienced colleagues, before being incrementally given greater responsibility.

Training and skills development were ramped up when more complicated mechanical tasks and involved knowledge-based work required more in-depth comprehension and faster acquisition of specific capabilities. Global spend per employee was increasing steadily between 2008 and 2019 to contend with the increased complexity of business issues as well as increasing skills development.[5] The "half-life" of job skills is constantly decreasing and was estimated by John Seely Brown to be only five years (meaning that after five years the skill is half as valuable) in 2016, with technical skills' half-life often even shorter.[6]

How are the newest labor market entrants hired by your company being prepared for these more demanding job functions? What knowledge transfer mechanisms and working frameworks have been created to enable their assimilation at your company? What workflow has been identified and processes developed to support successful achievement of their daily tasks and longer-term objectives?

Consider your own response to the increase in non-routine work over recent years—how have you adapted when your company has needed to modify direction and refocus resources quickly? What helped you improve how you approach and tackle unusual projects and unprecedented scenarios? Recognizing that now projects and pivots often involve complex, multidisciplinary, and multidimensional work, how are your experiences and learnings helping younger cohorts be effective in their work?

Remember Cary Bruce, Senior Vice President at EBSCO Information Services, who was designing the new work model for his region? Cary is a thoughtful, measured, and seasoned executive and natural manager—I know, because he was the CFO and CEO, respectively, and my immediate boss at two different companies where I worked in Germany from 1996 to 1998. He reads people well and supports their development and accomplishments, showing them how to work. His innate understanding as a manager came to the fore when his son, Nicolas, finished his master's degree and started his first-ever real job in Southern Germany at the beginning of March 2020.

Within two weeks of his starting, the German government announced a national lockdown. Nicolas was disappointed to be launching his professional career from home. Meanwhile, Cary was concerned that Nicolas would be neglected by his immediate supervisor and thereby disadvantaged in getting up to speed, asking quick questions as he settled into his new role. He also would not start building relationships that would support his professional growth through informal in-person encounters, nor could he absorb the company's culture and values. Cary was most worried that, isolated from his coworkers, his son would not be able to observe and adopt the functional skills he needed to complete tasks effectively.

From his own management experience, Cary was very aware of the need to give new, young hires structure and the building blocks of how to work—developing and supporting the relevant processes for their work. Nicolas was facile with digital applications and could use productivity tools; however, he was also launching his working life without a framework to guide him, focus his attention, and channel his energies. With little to no personal guidance and without a structured environment to confirm his progress, Cary saw evidence that Nicolas could flounder.

Long-established work practices used to be highly structured routines, clearly defined by time, space, title, and function. Most people's workdays had a fixed beginning, end, building, and department, with an assigned and tightly defined set of tasks that barely changed from week to week, month to month, and year to year.

Not so now. The workday has few fixed and defining boundaries, as application-rich smartphones allow location-independent interactions day and night across different media and multiple channels. The content and composition of work often changes from project to project, including different scope, length, size of team, and tasks involved. Oversight and protocols can change depending on the project leader, who, if seasoned in their field, may not be aware that newer hires might need to learn the mechanics of work and may not purposefully generate boundaries and milestones for them.

Cary knew younger employees' workflow management challenges would be exacerbated in working-from-home situations. As a caring father, he created a PowerPoint presentation with Nicolas's input to review, with tips about goal setting, task prioritization, and milestone achievement. He scheduled weekly virtual "management meetings" to recap and review accomplishments and learnings together so Nicolas could acquire the process knowledge and establish effective work habits.

Cary helped his son conceive an effective personal workflow framework that allowed Nicolas to advance his tasks, monitor his progress to stay on track, and meet each deadline. Within weeks, the frequency of meetings dropped. Nicolas's work skills developed as he refined his optimal working profile with form that allowed flexibility to respond to business needs, and he found his rhythm. End result: a proud father and a productive son who was set up for success at work. Admittedly, Nicolas still had to manage the isolation of repeated lockdowns over the following months.

Guidance, building blocks, and useful methodologies offer support without undermining someone's confidence and abilities. Do you have any subdued micromanaging tendencies—which possibly show up under stress? We often do! The key is to communicate clearly: business, project, and task objectives, as well as critical path elements, core principles, budget specifics, acceptable risk profiles, and where outer acceptable boundaries are.

Your preferred methodology of completing a task may well not suit the style, skills, and context of your team members. So it pays to remember the words of management guru Peter Drucker: "Knowledge workers *have* to manage themselves. They have to have *autonomy*."[7] However, I recognize that yielding power feel destabilizing and even nerve-racking, especially during these liminal times.

Oliver Nelson-Smith, Analyst at UK Finance, an organization that represents firms in the banking and finance industries in the United Kingdom, noted that the youngest cohorts "often feel anxious about asking questions," especially in a competitive sector.[8] Oliver therefore purposefully gives clear detail to reduce incidents of their independently finding Googled solutions that are "close enough or more or less in the right area." Instead, he advises them to "take a moment and think about what is the purpose of the task you have been asked to do and what is the context for it," as he has learned to do. He also shares ideas and improvements during collaborative work sessions, as well as encouraging and reacting positively to clarifying questions.

Yes, younger employees may well not accomplish the tasks how you would have done or how you would like. It can take an empathetic pause (or gulp!) for senior leaders to accept that younger employees also bring new perspectives and technical expertise. Remember, the "how" of work is changing, which entails exploring new methods and means. Your team members may utilize new techniques, approaches, or applications, which can bring new insights and learnings to benefit your business.

Rewarding Performance

Reviewing research and widespread corporate practices, performance metrics rarely align with companies' value creation, particularly with the emphasis shifting dramatically from manual to knowledge work.[9] Labor productivity is the ratio of output of goods and services to the labor hours devoted to production of that output and performance,[10] and it was Peter Drucker who first highlighted "the challenge in making knowledge work productive."[11] The traditional emphasis on measuring productivity is, as Dom Price, Work Futurist at Atlassian, puts it, "a great measure for machines" and is not balanced or recognizing human-centric factors such as mental health and burnout.[12] Dom promotes "finding measures for effectiveness, belonging, connectivity and thinking about things like innovation, creativity, and curiosity, which are important, lead indicators for a business—having a more rounded view of how we think about humans."

Consider carefully the metrics for performance that promote quality individual and team outcomes and also feed into the motivation cycle for your employees. Furthermore, pay attention to Key Performance Indicators, or KPIs, which may become outdated—and even irrelevant—during rapidly changing business conditions. Frequent check-ins suit unpredictable and accelerated business cycles and assist employees at all levels. This new coaching-style management also allows adjustments for updates and unforeseen circumstances and facilitates the performance of remote workers.

Elias Baltassis, Partner and Director at BCG, a preeminent management consulting firm, discussed the multiple factors the company maps to assess every employee's performance for bonus calculation, promotion potential, and training needs.[13] These criteria span hard and soft skills and include critical weighting on upward feedback and people development.

Since rewards drive future behaviors, do your current incentives align with company values and reward collaboration, cooperation, and other outcomes of the successful practice of empathy habits? Do you tailor recognition to have the most impact on each employee? A private note for one might be most meaningful, versus a group shout-out for another.

Voice and Value

To adjust for business conditions, the need for greater responsiveness has flattened hierarchies (reduced, not eradicated, layers) and driven multiple disciplines into collaborative meetings to debate ideas and test prototypes. The benefits of drawing on a wider range of thinking and expertise have increased to tackle more complex issues. Furthermore, there is greater need to engage younger employees who are primed to participate and bring fresh opinions and ideas, less encumbered by entrenched routines. However, inclusive collaboration across wide age differences often requires empathetic support to start productive discussions and maximize outcomes.

We have all observed starkly different points of view across the employee spectrum that have led to some less harmonious interactions that undermined performance and results. Some of the most dramatic disconnects are seen across generations, with frustration, impatience, and misinterpretation rife in communications, particularly between Baby Boomers—born between 1946 and 1964—and Millennial or Generation Z employees (Millennials were born between 1980 and 1995; Generation Z was born between 1995 and 2015).

"We tried bending our Millennials to our Boomer way of doing things!" Sarah laughed, but she was concerned. "But it simply hasn't been working." As CEO and owner of a toxic waste clean-up company, Sarah was frustrated about the continuing tensions between the Boomers and Millennials at her company. Conflicts had started to affect their culture, as well as productivity.

"What do they want?" I asked.

"What do you mean, 'What do they want?'!" Sarah responded, "When I started work, no one cared what I thought or what I wanted!"

"Yes, I remember that too," I agreed. "Is there currently much integration between the generational groups? Younger folks tend to engage when they can share their ideas and contribute."

"We aren't set up like that. The Millennials are the ones working on the frontline cleaning up the hazardous waste. Our management is all Boomers. The Leadership Committee is too, and that's where all the ideas, strategies, and operational plans are discussed," she explained.

I asked more about how the company operated and found out that the manager of the younger crew was both a Boomer and a veteran. I guessed that his military training was a bonus in terms of process and safety protocols when dealing with toxic waste. At the same time, I imagined he might also have a traditional command-and-control leadership style that might not be received so well by the younger team if they were looking to be empowered, learn, and grow.

"Maybe one of the Millennials—say, an emerging leader—could be invited to join the Leadership Committee?" I offered.

"I wouldn't want to single just one of them out." Sarah shook her head. "Actually, I had high hopes for one young woman, but recently she really disappointed me."

"Why? What happened? What did she do? Or what didn't she do?"

"I thought she would be a rock star. But, she just didn't get things done."

"That's a shame. Did she know specifically what your expectations were?"

Sarah paused. "I'm not sure she did." She thought for a second. "Now, come to think of it, she did make a comment about that."

Sarah had bought into the toxic waste clean-up franchise a dozen years ago and had achieved good growth year over year since then. The generational disconnect was something new, and it was affecting the company's prospects. She had exhausted all the management methods she knew.

We talked a long time and she asked many questions. She empathized. She shifted her orientation and put herself in the shoes of her Millennial employees and understood their world much better. She realized that it would help to explain in more detail to less-experienced employees what she needed done, considering significant ongoing changes. If she had particular specifications, she could communicate them. Her direct report might also have some ideas, which could be incorporated too.

To elevate empathetic understanding and communication across generational groups, Sarah made three major changes:

- INTEGRATION: An emerging Millennial leader was brought on to the Executive Leadership Committee to represent the younger employees. They shared ideas coming from the frontlines, generated by their interactions with customers. Boomer management valued their contributions, and the Millennials appreciated being heard and seeing their suggestions put into action.

- COACHING: A new performance management approach introduced weekly check-ins, especially for the less-seasoned employees. These conversations gave them frequent support to navigate new business conditions, as well as develop their skills, which Sarah found they were keen to do.

- RELATIONSHIPS: Two Millennials were put in charge of creating social events to nurture an integrated community across the company. They created fun occasions that everyone could participate in and that all employees enjoyed, creating shared memories and generating new bonds and understanding.

These simple, but critical, steps closed the gaps and integrated the alienated groups. The key was creating a more inclusive and empathetic environment that started to solicit and act upon the insights and ideas of people who had felt excluded. The younger employees now had a voice, a place at the leadership table, and their inputs were valued. The older employees heard the new ideas coming from the frontlines and respected their younger colleagues more. The corporate culture improved, as did intergenerational communication and cooperation, and productivity increased.

Here, the excluded group comprised younger employees, but this is certainly not always the case. Empathizing across all employees to integrate and include everyone is important for enabling people to engage and contribute fully. I would also like to both recognize and peel back the labels, as we are each and all certainly individuals first, with different personalities, backgrounds, and dimensions that determine the wholeness and uniqueness of who we each are. Labels are generally disliked, can have pejorative overtones, and are often counterproductive, since they may be untrue as often as they are true.

As mentioned in the previous chapter, an aspect of diversity and inclusion focuses on age distinctions, biases, and issues. Successful, sustainable work environments support people working together across all personal dimensions and contexts, recognizing and valuing what each person brings to the table and giving them a real or virtual chair. To engage every employee, empathy helps ensure everyone's ideas are invited, welcomed, and debated—from all races, age groups, expertise or experience levels, and other dimensions.

Technology Intuition

The blend of experience and expertise is worth addressing, specifically when it comes to technology, with the heavy weighting of digitalization in Future-of-Work environments that has elevated technical skills and understanding and increased utilization and dependency in every solution developed.

The different confidence and comprehension levels of employees about technology matters. Whether we were introduced (for example, Gen Xers like myself) or raised (for example, my Gen Z children) with particular technologies typically determines our interactions and relationships. My devices and applications are generally functional, useful adjuncts, facilitating my life. My son and daughter have a more fluid, investigatory, and experiential relationship with their hardware and software. Technology was already totally infused into their lives pre-COVID-19, with blurred distinction between "real" and "virtual" social interactions.

My comments are not about anyone's competence, but the effect of different technology education, experimentation, recreation, and intuition. With more time to browse, play, and explore innumerable applications' features and functionality on their devices, younger workers tend to have an intuitive understanding of technology. Older employees, who did not get a digital education at school (including older Millennials) or were not raised with easy access to digital devices, likely do not have the same aptitude or approach to technology. They therefore may have a different capacity to imagine what possibilities technology could afford your business, what new advances might bring, and how any of it might be applied.

So what? Consider your organization's current relationship with technology compared with 2019, before the pandemic. How many more processes or tasks are digitized or utilize technical capabilities to optimize, speed up, or reconfigure how you reach or serve your customers, as well as streamline workflow and facilitate synchronous and asynchronous virtual communication, freeing up people's time and improving safety aspects? How much more data is your business gathering to inform decisions in close to real time?

For most sectors going forwards, success requires up-to-date technology embedded into operations using different platforms and applications to interconnect with customers, vendors, and employees. Indeed, there is a great benefit to embracing the knowledge of even the youngest workers and their inherent technology "expertise," fluid acceptance, and comfort, and combining this with the depth of understanding and experience of older employees (who may be less technically adept).

Integrating and benefiting from the collective brain trust of your organization allows your business to develop the most innovative solutions and make the most informed, thoughtful decisions that combine expertise and experience to enhance and sustain your competitive edge. Everyone adds value, and empathy can help you sense specifically how well different workers understand technical developments, functions, and feature options; what perspectives may be at odds; and how to help colleagues work together productively.

Oliver Nelson-Smith told me, "Classic work hierarchies don't work well anymore. There isn't the same respect for the people higher up in the organization, as younger people are more and more aware that the person who is managing you, who might be paid much more than you, doesn't actually understand the tool anywhere near as well as you do."[14]

Many older employees in senior roles are often not fully aware of changing hierarchical dynamics nor the advantage of inviting the least experienced employees in the company into deliberations, especially about new technologies. Practicing empathy skills enables leaders at every level to consider how best to integrate and accommodate changing workplace dynamics and how to introduce new modes of operating, just as Sarah did. Introducing intergenerational, bi-directional mentoring pairs provides additional beneficial conduits for employees to share business experiences, technology understanding, and work-related nuances that bolster comprehension and confidence. These deliberate connections also build cross-company relationships and facilitate mutual empathizing between colleagues.

At the same time, attracting and retaining younger employees now depends on a digitally integrated approach to your business and an up-to-date technology stack as a base minimum. They are astutely aware of key tools workers need to be effective, how essential it is to collect and incorporate customers' data and feedback, and if the Customer Journey is competitive—for example, is your online customer interface using current user experience (UX) design, and are the features offered compelling?

Moreover, as consumers and employees, your youngest cohorts are highly attuned to the importance of advanced technologies for a business to sustain its advantage. This is another reason the base minimum state of digitalization of your business—and being at least on par with your competitors—is also an integral "must have" for the Employee Journey of younger employee groups. Anyone should be concerned about the viability of an organization that does not have an adequate digital platform to compete effectively.

Well-Being

The pace of technology developments has also affected us psychologically. The speed can seem relentless. The frequent iterations can feel overwhelming. The need for ongoing updates can feel destabilizing. Added to which, the pandemic brought extraordinary emotional strain, terrible tragedies, widespread burnout, unsettling uncertainty, and greater geography-based anomalies and volatilities.

How are you doing? No, seriously. What's been going on this week? Did anything distract you temporarily so you were not able to apply your full attention to your work? Were you worrying about a simmering issue at home? Was your inconsistent workout routine troubling you? Have you been stressing about any recent changes at work and what they might mean for your job or security? Were you fretting about saving for your kids' college? Did you wonder how you could help your friend or cousin who is struggling with anxiety?

At the same time, work-wise, maybe you have you been mulling over a potential alert relating to a current project:

- A coworker was less responsive than normal—did that signify anything?

- You witnessed an insensitive interaction at a meeting—how should you follow up?

- One of your reports dropped the ball again. Something small, but it feels like a red flag—how can you discreetly check what is going on?

Each of your company's employees has their own selection of these matters to register, assess, and decide if and what action to take before they are put aside and concentration is regained. So many of these issues are human-related, relying on empathy skills to figure out what should be done next. For work-related situations, the more your organization can reduce distracting stressors on employees, the easier it is for everyone to engage effectively in their work.

General concern and support for employees' mental, physical, and economic health had been rising before we were hit with a multi-year global health crisis. In 2013, the correlation between wellness and engagement was demonstrated in a study, with a high-engagement group of employees having higher psychological well-being and a low-engagement group exhibiting higher emotional exhaustion and depersonalization.[15] Meanwhile, reports of incidents of mental ill health at work had increased significantly—for example, in the United Kingdom in 2019, 72 percent of large organizations (over 250 employees) noted rises in mental health conditions.[16]

Alarm bells ringing back in 2020 about mental health being a potential second pandemic may have sounded overly dramatic. However, the onslaught of isolation and overwhelm spanning months, plus furloughs, firings, and cratered travel and hospitality sectors and freelance work projects, followed by new bouts of change with office recalls, pushbacks, and re-dos, has been tough at best. Early in the pandemic in 2020, people experienced increased stress (67 percent) and anxiety (57 percent) and were emotionally exhausted (54 percent).[17] Mid-2021, 76 percent of full-time US workers reported one or more mental health conditions over the previous twelve months—a sharp increase from 59 percent in 2019.[18] During this transformational period, a grounding, critical sense of stability and serenity is important to create through cultural connection and community.

Emphasis on employee well-being is a cornerstone of an empathetic core culture—tapping into what people are going through. With a comprehensive 360-degree approach to wellness, well-being, and benefits, empathy can help recognize possible mental health issues; encourage safe, open dialogue; and provide focused support. A human-centric approach means customizable wellness offerings that employees can tailor to their specific needs and lifestyle.

Mental health is now probably the most pressing area to discuss openly in destigmatized ways, along with other well-being topics. Leaders can be aware of and watch for early signals while providing a variety of resources encompassing confidential access to in-person and online support. Physical health is a second important pillar where a wide range of alternatives for employees can be offered such as gym memberships, yoga classes, and nutrition coaching. Financial instability has also been identified as a major source of agitation and tension, so financial health is advisable to add to your employee well-being program, if it is not already offered.

Workforce groups in different offices, remote locations, and regions may be interested in different options. It is beneficial to survey employees to refine the selection and content, so your company is providing the desired benefits that are accessible for everyone. Meanwhile tracking usage and tallying comments allows offerings to be adapted and updated to best support all employees' well-being.

Upskilling Careers

What are your top three skills? (This is a tough one!) What are the next skills that you have identified to develop, and to what end? How is your employer helping you stay competitive? Are you exploring options to develop additional operational experience where you are now? No doubt you, and most other employees, are regularly distracted by these questions.

Younger workers in particular recognize the new realities of work, have flexible approaches to jobs and careers, and are aware of the need for frequent upskilling to stay relevant and competitive. The Future of Jobs Report 2020 from the World Economic Forum related that while the number of jobs destroyed will exceed the number of "jobs of tomorrow" created, job destruction has accelerated while job creation has slowed, and *50 percent of all employees* will need reskilling by 2025.[19] Their awareness understandably undermines their feeling of safety, which influences decisions they make about the companies they work for.

Recent hires often seek early confirmation about advancement, often leading to consternation about an inappropriate request for a promotion or a raise after only a few months. If you have fielded one or more of these, consider what the young employee might actually be thinking or mean to ask, "Do I have a future here?" (As well as, "Help me move out of my parents' home!") While your reaction may not be positive to the discussion, it did get you thinking! At the same time, since entry-level jobs are often significantly more complex than they were for previous generations, why would they not advance in less time?[20] Everything has sped up.

Technology developments have also catalyzed shifts in our career cartography. As hierarchies flatten to increase adaptability, vertical ladders are being replaced by responsive pathways that include horizontal and diagonal opportunities. One knock-on effect and benefit is that workers can now apply existing skills in new areas, as well as develop skills that offer new opportunities and career pathways. Indeed, "every individual should plan for having five careers over their lifetime," Helen Barrett wrote in the *Financial Times* in September 2017.[21]

Since careers are less linear and the future is less certain, all employees need to be proactively managing and monitoring their career progress themselves, supported by training, skills-tracking, upskilling, and offering of new role options. Employees who are advancing towards or navigating the peak of their earning potential and those who are reviewing and readjusting their career priorities looking towards retirement have different but related issues to consider. How is your current career being actively developed by your employer and managed by you?

Gary A. Bolles, author of *The Next Rules of Work*, urges, "Whatever door you need to come in through to get the insights about you, to understand what motivates you, the skills that you most love using, the problems that you most love solving, the kinds of people that help you to do your best work, and so on. Whatever helps you to get those insights and information, you should do. And keep on experimenting and trying different techniques. Because what works for you today might not work tomorrow. Then you have to tie that to agency, as you have to go find and create that work."[22]

Talent Mapping

Monitoring a real-time skills inventory of your organization—not a compilation of years' old resumes or outdated competencies—is now critical for staying on top of your business's current and projected skills needs. The Employee Journey is no longer a linear trajectory into and out of your organization, ending in retirement. Think instead about talent mapping and career cartography, with employees taking intersecting, overlapping, and networked pathways that bring people to, around, beyond, and even back into your company.

With a current skills inventory, each person's updated capabilities can be tracked and matched with new internal opportunities as business and skills needs evolve. To stay competitive, you and other employees also naturally want to acquire new skills and have new experiences that will eventually prompt a departure from your team, your division, or your company. Finding a new role within your organization is the best option to explore first. With a skills inventory and good network of relationships across your company, you can be alerted to, as well as discover, new opportunities for yourself and your reports. Work is a dynamic landscape and activity now.

Muriel Clauson, Co-founder of Anthill, in 2020 started to hear select leaders saying, "I actually want to make sure that our people don't leave our company unless it's absolutely the right thing for them, and that while they're here, we're helping them get the most out of work. We want them to be happier. We want to be able to shift people seamlessly to where they're best positioned to succeed."[23]

Why on earth did they leave?

You should never need to ask this question about one of your team members. Milestone moments provide revealing data, as departing employees in particular are often prepared to share most openly. Does your company's exit protocol include a reasonably detailed survey or interview? Acting upon shared admissions helps prevent further departures, so make a habit of discovering why anyone moves on.

Furthermore, if anyone ultimately wants to leave to explore other options and advance their career, do not stop empathizing. If there is not a good fit at your organization for them anymore, for whatever reason, consider the benefits of helping them find a new employer.

I am not kidding.

Employers who understand the significant—and increasing—benefits do. How much more likely are they to return to your company as a more accomplished and valuable worker with a broader skills base and operational range if you help them take their next step? At the very least, would it not also be a benefit to have them as a good ambassador for your company and your team, helping you hire new people in a competitive talent market?

Exiting your company is no longer the end of the relationship with the former employee. Firms sometimes still take the approach that "if you are no longer with us, you are dead to us." But now the world is too small, acquired corporate knowledge too valuable, intra-ecosystem relationships too important, and nurtured good talent too rare for a scorched-earth mindset.

Keeping in touch with and mapping former employees is wise as your business grows, needs adapt, and markets develop. Over time, people's multiple careers increasingly involve many different serial and simultaneous arrangements. Your organization will have opportunities to hire former employees and almost-hired strong candidates in many capacities. Consider how multi-year vesting agreements for company equity or options could be put on hold for a few years to keep connections strong and incentivize former employees to return.

Take frequent pulse surveys to find out how people are doing, including at every milestone, to allow your organization to confirm or adjust employees' experiences. Empathizing with each person through every step and phase of their Employee Journey with your firm strengthens and supports your competitive advantage.

Empathy Habits

1 **Employ optionality:** For every new hire, explore preferred and viable arrangements for both parties to improve engagement and outcomes.

2 **Share building blocks:** Give guidance and possible methods to help younger employees channel and be effective in their efforts.

3 **Bridge gaps:** Become a mentor, spanning generational or other gaps, to improve mutual understanding.

4 **Identify top skills:** Keep up to date with yours and others' key current and developing skills.

5 **Value voices:** Regularly ensure diverse voices are actively solicited and heard.

6 **Emphasize well-being:** Always remember self-care and team-care, promoting healthy routines—including regular meals and exercise.

7 **Orient towards strengths:** Allocate projects and tasks that support employees' engagement, performance, and growth.

8 **Support self-managed careers:** Periodically confirm your reports are monitoring their progress, and help them plan out possible next steps.

13

Sales
Selling with Empathy

"I'M NOT a huge advocate of empathy in the workplace," the
partner of a successful boutique merchant bank told me
in June 2021.

I expressed surprise. He was in the ultimate service business. "But don't you spend time trying to understand what
is going through your clients' minds and the world as they
see it? Don't you find it important to tap into what they are
going through?"

"Of course, that's what I do all day, every day," he replied.

"That's empathy!" I said. "You're using it every day in your
work."

Integrating empathy into your individual and team sales
routines—whether you are part of the sales or business development group or in a senior external-facing role—is crucial
to stay competitive. Empathy helps you stand out from the
crowd in faster-evolving, more complex, and increasingly
crowded markets.

Technology's advances—which have been driving extraordinary changes throughout the business world—have also

greatly influenced the dynamics of sales processes. The balance of power between buyers and sellers has shifted, the channels have changed, the discussions have deepened, the relationships are more important—with prospects and customers, and among sales team members.

What's more, COVID-19-triggered turmoil and hardship increased emotional instability and purchase hesitancy among consumers and businesses, which has lingered. Remember periods when you pulled back completely as a consumer and other times you made cautious or impulse buys as your moods swung? The engagement of target segments changed depending on evolving local restrictions, government support, vaccination levels, and waves of weariness, all of which affected prospects' sanity and security. (Re)assessing who your core customers are and "should" be is a crucial iterative exercise when uncertainties are particularly disruptive.

Even with renewed economic growth after the deep troughs of 2020, potential buyers and existing clients have understandable continuing wariness, feeling knock-on effects of supply chain disruptions and many marketplace uncertainties, including the possible impact of new virulent COVID-19 variants. Greater sensitivity to the nuances of clients' evolving situations is essential, recognizing their prevailing needs and oscillating emotional states. Otherwise, how can you offer them a relevant solution proposed in language that resonates with their current sentiment, acknowledges their challenges, pinpoints their key issues, and communicates the well-matched benefits of your offering?

Power Shift

There has been an important transfer of power. Sellers used to have more power. Buyers *needed* to interact with you as a key source of information about products and services they desired. Now, easy access to extraordinary amounts of data allows buyers to conduct extensive research, find countless detailed and verified opinions, and solicit specific recommendations.

Before you ever contact a potential buyer, they are now well advanced in the sales process, with much more knowledge about your offering *and* your competitors'. Recall what you did when you needed to find the perfect CRM solution, travel site, air-fryer oven, camera bag, or meditation app. You asked a couple of colleagues and a personal friend or two, and even got some help with research, to come up with a top ten list that you whittled down to three, all *before* ever connecting with a potential vendor.

The bar has been raised. To convert leads into sales, you have to understand enough details and nuances about a potential buyer's situation to confirm your offering is a good fit. Your business must be responsive to their initial reactions, concerns, issues, and ongoing changing needs. You also require that information to discern how, where, and when you should best share compelling differentiation about your offering and communicate these aspects convincingly.

Without the step of humanizing your desired customers, figuring out what their problems really are is nearly impossible. What are the pertinent perspectives and experiences of the person whom your organization needs to find, message, connect with, engage, interview, address, convert, and then serve, having persuaded them that your product or service is going to make their life easier? How can everyone fully understand the Customer Journey to coordinate operations effectively?

Using an empathy lens, it's simple. With the strategic benefit of creating target customer profiles to bring the person or people to life, once there is a believable person whom you could imagine meeting in the street, you can start to empathize with them. You can put yourself in your prospect's or existing client's shoes to think about and feel what they are going through and act in alignment with their needs and yours. Empathy allows you to tap into prospects' experiences and situations, develop lasting customer relationships, hire the right team members, and collaborate effectively to achieve optimal results.

"I know you're trying to figure out what clients want, but have you tried empathy?"

Customer Context

Who are your clients now and how have their profiles and needs been changing recently? Which target groups are emerging or clients' needs shifting, and which are worth pursuing? Where should the strategic focus be, based on the current and anticipated perspectives and experiences of prospects and customers, to achieve reasonably forecastable sustainable growth? These questions are worth asking with reasonable frequency—as we plan, build, and manage through the reverberations after a huge global shock—to determine the dynamics of relevant sectors and regions. Regular updates from sales reps keep adding texture and relevant context to your target customer profiles.

In your research, before you have any contact with prospects and can ask any detailed questions, what do you imagine they are thinking about? What are their concerns? What key issues are they facing? What is happening in their world? Gathering these details adds beneficial depth to the information others may already have or are collecting. The data improve the relevance of your outreach as you empathize more, understanding the nuances and complex realities that your potential buyers are dealing with.

Starting with general economic circumstances and specific supply chain constraints, gather industry and local intelligence. Since empathy starts with you, awareness of your own changing wants, needs, emotional drivers, and triggers is useful to remind you of the THINK, FEEL, and ACT steps to employ and find out what is transpiring for others. You can empathize better if you understand how your contact feels about their situation, their business, and themselves, both professionally and personally.

What can you find out about their particular company, its positioning and circumstances? How did their business fare during the initial waves of the pandemic? How well have they been doing since then? These details help you assess how they are adjusting to new, more digitized operational environments that may well affect the relevance of your company's products or services.

People want to be understood and valued, and if a potential customer senses you care about their situation and respect them, a relationship can develop. Scott Schiller, Global Chief Commercial Officer at Engine Group, a data-driven marketing solutions company, said, "Whenever you are talking to a customer, you must be empathetic and intelligent about their business. Doing so will gain the customer's trust that you want to address their needs. Thorough preparation requires research about the person, the company, the industry, competitors, and challenges. The mistake many client-facing executives make most often (regardless of their experience level) is to talk about themselves and their company rather than focusing on the customer."[1]

What are the potential buyer's current choices and challenges? What stressors are they facing in their business situation? What do you know of internal dynamics within their division or team? What emotional state are they in and why? How can any solution you provide ease any of their issues and smooth any operational road bumps to improve their competitive advantage?

An empathetic approach focusing on the potential buyer means drawing out the conversation and listening actively. These actions strengthen this first critical connection and start to build trust, leading to more sharing as the person feels safe to open up, yielding insights about what problems you might be able to help them with. Remember to keep updating the texture and scope of your potential buyer's profile as they provide more specifics about their situation, which may change during the—possibly extended—sales cycle.

Mutually Matched

To help you figure out the fit with your potential buyer, ask: Where are you aligned personally and professionally? What cultural values do your companies share? What points of commonality can you discover and demonstrate to help them get comfortable with you and allow initial conversations to flow smoothly?

Phrase and position your initial messaging; carefully interpret correspondence and follow up appropriately, being sensitive to their signals and cues as discussions evolve. Ramon Ray, Editor and Founder of Smart Hustle, a platform that inspires and educates small business founders, is a high-energy, entertaining entrepreneur, podcaster, and moderator. He was contacted by a large European brand, who asked him, "Ramon, we know you eat burned pancakes and bacon! Could you come and host our event?" He told me, "That was one of the best examples of a company who gets me. They know who they are dealing with, and that's what they want."[2]

However, being empathetic does not necessarily mean that when you act, you are the only one modifying your behavior. Empathy also helps you realize how to communicate your preferred work style and encourage an effective working relationship. When Ramon was pursuing another opportunity, he told me, "The guy kept saying 'Ramon, can you call me, can you call me, can you call me?' Maybe he was an older gentleman and that was just his thing. However, I was sensing I needed to get the deal done by email. My calling him and answering the same questions by email was not a fit.

"So I gently shared, 'To serve you better, here are the answers to your questions. Do you mind shooting me one or two emails so we can get through this?' Guess what? We sealed a big speaking deal. I was able to share with him how I prefer to work and explained 'I can serve you better if you give me a little chance.' And he did and we moved forward. It was important to me to say, 'Give me a minute, can you just come to my side?' And he did!" Ramon exhaled with his affable laugh.[3]

Your empathetic exchanges help you confirm if there is a sufficiently good overall match. If there is not, you do not want to waste their time—or yours—trying to force a fit. Otherwise, all parties end up dissatisfied, often with distracting fallout.

Getting to Yes

When you are ready to make your pitch, incorporating all the data that you have gathered, you can craft a highly targeted and relevant presentation, demonstrating you heard your potential buyer and understand their particular situation well. Using a format and lexicon they are comfortable with, you can recognize the challenges they are facing, what (they believe) their needs are, and how your offering is a realistic and compelling solution. Remember to address relevant issues that convincingly counter any points of resistance that you identified through your empathetic exchanges—for their attention as well as their superiors'.

Robert Birge, Chief Growth Officer at ASOS, told me, "Whatever it is that is actually useful to them at any given point, just try to be useful at every stage without trying to over-engineer or create a rational argument that is going to persuade someone. Be useful all the way through. Keep asking yourself, 'Is this useful to them?'"[4]

They also need to know you can fulfill their internal reporting requirements and validating metrics if you clinch the deal. Hazel Lyons, International Advertising Director at Travel Weekly USA, uses empathy to be highly attuned to servicing clients' needs, providing numerically weighted proposals and reports that respond to a focus on return on investment.[5] Sales professionals at companies selling large, complex, long-term bundles—such as software platform and application developers—sometimes develop the business case for their prospect to get the internal approval they need to confirm the sale.

Your empathy skills may need to be fully engaged if you are communicating the benefits for an end user who is distant or disconnected from the person you are selling to, especially if they have very different points of view and experiences. Jeroen de Kempenaer of Philips Engineering Solutions is often working on innovations for clients who are not connected with the customers they serve. One such project was developing novel components for medical wearables that are manufactured by a company selling to doctors who prescribe them to patients.

There may be more than one type of potential customer to satisfy. Jeroen also deals with many situations where multiple customers need consideration throughout the pitching and providing process. Each must be understood and empathized with. "In the healthtech market, we have to serve three customers who are equally important: The doctors must be happy with the technical results from our new widget. Staff must be happy using it because very often the doctor won't use it. Staff will use it. And the doctor will look at the results. And the patient. In the end, if the experience for the patient is good, then the whole pathway will be a lot easier."[6]

Do not forget to address the emotional element, integrating the empathetic understanding of the person or people and their motivations. Why? "A final purchase decision—at that moment of conversion—is very rarely a rational decision. It's non-rational, it's more emotive," as Robert Birge stressed.[7] Yes, people need the rational justification, but the moment they buy, the moment the scales tip in your favor, is likely emotionally driven. Intersecting in the process, Robert clarified, "Think about that context: 'how can I be useful to you?' Which means 'have you helped me envision what I am going to feel like when I have it?'" Rather than any explanation, it is the positive, imagined experience that stimulates the conversion.

Empathy can give you critical attunement as you approach a potential sale. The person might feel awkward explaining a convoluted decision-making process at their company, embarrassed or frustrated about a boss who micromanages signoffs, or anxious about a seemingly minor issue that conceals a deeper concern. It is essential to draw them out and discover what moves and matters to them, as well as what pressures they are under. You need to assuage or convert their negative feelings to positive sentiment about your offering with compelling counters, supported by your nurtured connection and emotive anecdotes, or you will not get the outcome you want.

These benefits extend through completion of the sale. Your deeper empathetic connection and thoughtful understanding of your new customer's challenges allow you to continue confirming there is a good fit for your product or service that will be appreciated after purchase. Implementation can then also be finely tuned to suit needs well, improving the positive reception and results and keeping your new client satisfied.

Customer Service

Because, of course, the signature on the dotted line is just the beginning of a new, important phase that must be consistent with all prior communications and interactions. Initial dialogues with prospects and post-conversion conversations with them as new clients are reciprocal. Anna Persin, Co-founder of recruiting firm Holker Watkin Limited, pointed out, "It's two-way because your client is also testing you."[8] In recruiting, you might have landed the project, but the sales process keeps going as promising candidates are shared with the client who assesses both the possible hire *and* the recruiter for how well the client's needs have been captured and manifested in the person presented.

Are you sure you understand what your new customers want? Robert Birge pointed out that by heavily emphasizing great empathetic customer service, people may miss the point. Instead, making sure the product works or the service delivers might be a better focus of efforts, rather than having empathetic people offer comfort when customers' basic needs are not satisfied.[9]

Similarly, do customers know what they really want? Have they thought through all the salient details? With clients from recruiting to innovation, empathetic and adept management during this delicate phase of product trial or service execution is crucial. In the service business, it is particularly important to be in tune with your customers' specific objectives in order to achieve the experience—the satisfaction—they are expecting. Detailed parameters may need carefully clarifying and honing *while* the service is being provided, for which empathy is an important skill for managing the client dynamics successfully.

Consider an executive search project for which the initial desired profile—experience and competencies—necessarily evolves and is refined as candidates are vetted. To acknowledge the unrealistic promise of fulfilling a client's *entire* wish list, Anna Persin's process presented a selection of candidates for a client to rank. Then a benchmarking process was necessary to reveal their priorities, anticipating potential trade-offs.

This delicate exercise uncovers, as well as crystallizes, the client's preferences—and they continue to assess the recruiter's understanding and alignment. Other types of scoring systems and calibration techniques are used across different services to refine definition with additional details. This clarification is especially important for understanding qualitative elements of the client's desires and needs for which everyone participating has different perceptions, elevating empathy skills' usefulness.

The ongoing sales process also involves tighter relationships along the supply chain, for which management can best bring an empathetic and collaborative approach. For example, software companies' customers have been asking, even demanding, to be involved in their vendors' research and development process with a desire (aka intent) to influence the prioritizing of new features and even suggest new functionality. These clients are the ultimate frontline for the software itself.

In 2019, I witnessed the close community of software developer Workfront's executives' and account managers' friendly and absorbed discussions with their clients. They listened very attentively, trying to figure out how their software was being used and stress-tested in the field and how and where it could be improved to serve end users better, as well as what was needed most urgently.

Relying on Relationships

The head of one sales group in the New York office of a European financial services company estimates 90 percent of his teams' sales are relationship-based. He only hires people with a genuine interest in others and a well-developed ability to connect with them. To stand out, developing meaningful rapport with possible customers is essential, especially as the sales cycle becomes more involved. Relationships are so important now that in many companies, if you made the sale, you may now stay on the account team to bring the benefits of the connection you cultivated and share (appropriately) the plethora of insights you gained about the new client.

The pandemic caused a substantial decrease in business travel, so in-person meetings are not as frequent. The merchant bank partner told me that a reduced number of future trips would be focused entirely on building or nurturing relationships, unencumbered by distracting but necessary operational details. Logistics and other administrative matters would be handled via digital correspondence going forwards.

Since it can be hard now to generate a reason for yet another video call, stimulating deeper relationships has become crucial starting from the initial contact. Whenever you are following up, lean into the common connections and ensure you are frequently reminding your potential buyer about mutual commonalities and showing personal interest, reinforcing the reason why they want to continue interacting with you—especially in comparison to someone else with whom they do not connect in the same way.

It is much more enjoyable to combine business with pleasure, when meetings do not feel as much like work. A video call can be a chance for a client to convey some work-related development or frustration, as well as share an amusing anecdote or personal passion. Meanwhile, you can be alerted early to relevant developments and find out more about the mechanics and status of their business.

Meaningful relationships are easier to develop online now that we are used to "visiting" people in their homes via video calls, gathering more information about them in unobtrusive ways. When there is mutual exposure—both parties giving windows into their personal lives—it fosters a foundation for trust and more willingness to share likes and dislikes, interests and hobbies.

Furthermore, sales meetings, forced to go virtual in 2020 and 2021, were unexpectedly effective, so a significant portion are staying virtual. Research in 2021 by HubSpot found that 63 percent of sales leaders believe virtual sales meetings are equally or more effective than traditional, face-to-face meetings.[10] Empathy can be helpful for promoting easy conversation flow, rather than relying on a chat over drinks.

For in-person activities, to develop bonds with prospects, find out what they really enjoy doing, watching, attending, or visiting. What sport activity, entertainment outing, music concert, comedy club, cultural event, or venue do they appreciate most? This is where your preferences *and* theirs should be well aligned. Your relationship will be enhanced if you are doing something together where you both have authentic and enthusiastic pleasure or even passion. The enjoyment creates mutual connection, as well as important shared, positive memories. Feigned interest would soon be discovered and would undermine carefully nurtured trust.

There may be limitations on what you can to do to strengthen your relationships with prospects because of cost or regulation, as is the case in financial services. A senior financial trader told me she builds relationships based on carefully tailored, client-specific experiences that must also be compliant with company policy and regulations. She got approval to take a client and their child to a baseball game after discovering that both their kids adored baseball. These events that allow her to create special ties combine with her regular calls, during which she always takes time at the beginning for personal discussion, reminding her client of their well-established connection, as well as cultivating the relationship further. She also benefits from this initial interaction because it allows her to tap into their emotional state and assess receptivity to new opportunities before she launches into any business discussion.

Maintaining relationships with existing clients also means checking in periodically. A new development might potentially affect their need and use of your product or service and what upsells might be relevant and when. Indeed, the circumstances of all integrated members along your supply chain continue to be in flux—from your vendors to your clients and beyond to their customers as well—which are all important for you to stay on top of.

Team Talk

The "lone wolf" image of a successful salesperson is outdated in the current environment. Brian Bresee of HubSpot confirms that the most successful teams collaborate.[11] Managers are coached to promote psychological safety using inclusive language, so every team member can feel comfortable enough to communicate and collaborate openly and support each other's successes and boost team outcomes. Brian pairs up his teams' members to share skills, which also increases dialogue and cooperation and deepens their mutual understanding. Similarly, at cloud communications provider Fuze, sales team members confer after every call to explore how they can help others make progress and convert sales, improving overall team results.[12] Within teams, there are high levels of mutual respect, supported by strong interpersonal relationships.

For Scott Schiller of Engine Group, "Building trust is the core of all this. I think you build trust by helping the team understand the longer-term approach to the business. Collaboration comes in many forms: sharing approaches, successes, and failures amongst the group. Most salespeople can't help but compete against each other. Doing so is a wasted effort because we live in a very fluid environment. A salesperson's success does not diminish someone else's potential success."[13]

The head of a financial sales group practices a different empathy-related strategy, deliberately maintaining his own clients so that he can connect well with his teams' daily experiences and support them better. His conviction about empathy's positive effect on performance drives the incentive model he uses for his team. Only 50 percent of someone's bonus is based on their financial performance; the rest is determined by how well they use their interpersonal skills to develop strong relationships—both externally *and* internally.

Setting team goals encourages everyone to understand the benefit of building off each other's ideas and skills. Group targets also incentivize members of your sales team to collaborate thoughtfully and strategically, as well as support each other. Each person has strengths in different areas; for instance, one might have a particularly compelling turn of phrase to encourage or convince prospects who are hesitant about a specific feature.

Keep It Real

Authenticity is all the more important now for establishing and sustaining credibility in any outwardly facing role— whether sales-focused, working on business development, or negotiating strategic partnerships. Communicating "you" as you are allows another to connect properly, without inconsistencies that could undercut their tentative trust in you and your nascent relationship.

In contrast, if a potential buyer's belief in you is shaken during the sales process, it is unlikely they will ever convert. Any destabilizing requires much time and effort to reassure an apprehensive or disenchanted customer, never mind possible unwanted negative comments on social media channels. Imagine their state of mind if they feel they have been lied to: What else was not true?

Furthermore, in dynamic business conditions, definitive pronouncements can shake confidence. Uncertainties are a given. A more convincing way of earning someone's trust is to be transparent about your offering's current functionality or features, with realistic projections about future developments. The strength of your standing is validated when they can feel reassured that if they buy from you, you will be open with information they need to know about in a timely manner. Empathy brings the point home, especially at an organization consistently focused on the Customer Journey.

Empathy Habits

1 **Do more research:** For every outreach, gather the data necessary to make a good initial impression.

2 **Listen actively:** Find out as much as possible about your prospect by asking questions and listening carefully.

3 **Find common ground:** Make a habit of small talk to find experiences and interests you share so you can deepen the connection.

4 **Nurture relationships:** Regularly follow up, finding activities to do or interests to follow together to strengthen the bond, build trust, and cultivate loyalty.

5 **Share insights:** Benefit from collaboration across the team by comparing success stories and cautionary tales.

14

Leadership
Transitioning from Commander to Coach

"I'M BEING told now to cater to my individual team members' preferences—to adjust for them in terms of where they want to work and how. But, my preference is that everyone comes into the office. What about *my* preferences?!"

It was March 2021, and I had just given a virtual speech about "Succeeding in the Future of Work" to an audience of corporate leaders and executives. I was fielding submitted questions, and this one came from Anthony.

I heard him. I heard both the annoyance and weariness in his words. Yes, it all *sounded* good for leaders to adapt empathetically to enable employees do their best work and produce the best results... until it was *his* company, *his* team, and the burden was on *him* to adapt to what team members wanted. I imagined that he did care what his team wanted, too. I imagined that he was open to adapting for some of their preferences. Up to a point.

But juggling home-working schedules? Dealing with the additional complexity of a dispersed team with colleagues often split between office and home? Knowing that a combination of scenarios would mean paying extra attention in order to not favor people working at the office, where he mostly was? Understanding that hybrid meetings meant "location independent" and continuing with everyone participating via Zoom? It was too much work, and to what end?

I sensed that Anthony felt previous office-based arrangements worked well enough. Yes, it had become more of a struggle working at a faster pace, with increasing project work of different types, but he stayed on top of things. He had found it very challenging to manage his work and team from home, although he had finally found a rhythm of sorts. When everyone was in the office, he managed to get his work done and keep an eye on everyone else. He challenged me to tell him his needs were not important.

"Of course, your preferences matter!" I said. "And your team's preferences matter too. Don't you need them to make things happen? This business climate is not easy. The more you incorporate their needs, the less distracted and better situated they can be, and the better able to concentrate and perform at higher levels, which improves *your* results. The compromises needed to achieve a reasonable balance of everyone's needs takes more effort to begin with, I agree. But, it's all worth it!"

Anthony was not convinced. "I prefer to have everyone together in the office where I can talk to them to assign projects, give them feedback, and build team spirit."

Old habits die hard because their worn grooves are familiar and feel effortless, even when they are out of date and insufficient to meet the raised bar. Establishing new, relevant habits is essential, especially for leaders, using periods of disruption to facilitate their launch. People are still figuring out adapted, effective work routines, and some strategic "nudges" can help shift their activities or approaches. Taking advantage of these liminal times is important if you are purposefully going to make the transformation necessary to update working practices fully at your company, within your division, department, or team.

New World "Order"

But it is not just about leaders giving more flexibility. It is also about giving more autonomy.

"I say it; you do it." Let's face it, for most of us, telling people what to do is easier, particularly if we have reasonable conviction about the wisdom and logic of our instructions. Which you do, right? As a thoughtful leader, why would you not? How could you not? We know—we believe we know or try to develop—the best way forwards, the appropriate next steps for our team, division, or organization.

Or we did.

Now, we are in a different boat on a different ocean. The new boat has better equipment and bigger sails and it goes faster. But the waves are bigger and the wind is stronger. We need every hand on deck ready to jibe if the wind changes and alert so they can adjust the sails' tautness as the winds' strength fluctuates.

New digitized business operations mean augmented customer connectivity, real-time feedback loops, and additional instantaneous channels of communication. As a result, the amount and speed of data being received from the marketplace has increased in parallel with customers' expectations that products and services will be updated quickly, therefore becoming a competitive necessity.

It simply takes too long to wait for data from the frontlines to be contextualized and reported up to management or for insights to percolate up before committees update strategies for dissemination. At the start of the COVID-19 pandemic, Norman de Greve explained how at CVS Health the next level of management was invited to participate on their executive leadership calls, leveling the hierarchies of communication, in order to gather more direct insights from them and be better able to understand customers' needs.[1]

Meanwhile, new upstarts were ready to skip into space left undefended if an incumbent had not pivoted in time or its executives' efforts to adapt were woefully slow. Solutions will be inadequate if corporations rely only on C-suite executives' understanding and experience, as the marketplace is changing much faster now. It would be very difficult for executives to have a sufficient understanding of innovations constantly coming online to consider which are relevant and what possibilities particular technologies could afford the company. Drawing on the collective brain power of an organization is at minimum desirable, if not essential, these days, especially when soliciting updates and inputs from workers who are closest to your customers.

How well has your company adapted to the new digitized business era so far? How flexible is your company's structure? How easily were operations modified and new capabilities launched since this period of inflection began? How well have senior executives shifted mindset and strategies, adapting for dramatically different and dynamic conditions? How have leaders throughout your organization responded, to generate and embrace new opportunities?

Moreover, are managers ready to reallocate people who are flexible about what they are focused on and encouraged to take on new assignments? Are people working close to customers able to assess new market data and share ideas within internal cross-functional teams who swiftly generate prototypes to explore new opportunities? Have leaders and managers adopted a flexible mindset yet to adjust for business conditions?

Operationally, hierarchical management mindsets and methods were cemented to conventional rigid and fixed organization structures that did not accommodate the new types of iterations that your company likely experienced since the COVID-19 crisis began. A more organic, responsive, and human-centered approach means leading the transition to a suppler, flatter framework that facilitates sharing responsibility more broadly across your company.

Areas to Emphasize

With clarified accountability, managers are being empowered to make timely decisions. Workflow can be reconfigured and redirected in a matter of weeks—or days—depending on business needs. Data can be circulated and utilized more efficiently. An updated approach from leaders absorbs the essential elements of empathy in order to delegate more to direct reports who are, in turn, pushing more accountability down and out to the edges of their organizations.

Practicing empathy, you are in a stronger position to decide how tasks should be allocated, what your team members are capable of, how they each handle pressure, what they are motivated by, what oversight is optimal for each person, what recognition individuals respond to, and how to coach them constructively. Integrate empathy in the following key areas of leadership, while also consistently infusing it into all your outward-facing and inward-focused interactions.

PURPOSE: Customers are increasingly discerning about the brands they identify and align with and what they buy. To gain and retain loyal customers, your leadership starts with enabling customers to understand and connect with the purpose of your business all along the Customer Journey. In KPMG's 2021 CEO Outlook, 87 percent of CEOs said purpose is central to building their brand reputation.[2] Similarly, articulate your organization's purpose and engage employees empathetically by connecting them with the meaning of their work. Globally, 64 percent of CEOs in 2021 cited their organization's main objective was to embed purpose into decisions they make in everything they do. Hidden agendas can divert attention and fragment the forward momentum of your organization or group. Does your company have a clearly defined and articulated purpose?

CULTURE: Corporate culture and values have a profound effect on everyone in the organization, as well as influence potential and existing buyers' attitudes and interest. Major environmental and socio-political issues, such as climate change action and diversity and inclusion, are critical for companies to incorporate and stress in their value sets and concerns. In 2020, Mark Read of WPP made this commitment: "We are going to publish our diversity date and set ourselves targets and be accountable. It's a mixture of leadership, communication, transparency, and target setting."[3] In 2021, 58 percent of global CEOs said they face greater demand from stakeholders for more reporting on Environmental, Social, and Governance (ESG) issues.[4]

Leaders are stewards of the corporate culture and ensure that the values are clearly understood and reinforced daily across the company. Leadership is responsible for translating what each value means in terms of employee behavior—at the office, working remotely, and on trips to see clients. Certain divisions, locales, and teams may have cultural particularities; however, these aspects are best variations of the existing cultural tenets. Emphasize the key values of open-mindedness, inclusion, and empathy. These values foster trust, reaffirm employees' value, promote active participation in the organization, and manifest behavior for everyone to mirror in all their interactions. Culture is actively lived, or it languishes.

TRUST: Trust is essential for workers to feel psychological safety and a sense of belonging. Trust is necessary for employees to be comfortable taking innovative risks. That trust starts with you. Trust is also a reciprocated experience which cultivates mutual confidence and comfort so that you are prepared to cede more responsibility to each team member. Frances McLeod of Forensic Risk Alliance, discussing the company's culture and the partners' relationships with employees who are distributed across the United States and Europe, working from home and eight offices, said, "The moment reciprocity goes away, the relationship is compromised."[5]

You can increase trust and engage employees more by giving them more autonomy as well as more choice about their work.[6] In addition, expressing some vulnerability and asking for help as a leader, you generate more cooperation from your team, stimulating trust in them and encouraging them to share their own concerns, issues, and observations in return. With solid empathetic relationships, you can test what your reports are ready for, get more open feedback about progress, and adjust appropriately as necessary. Relationships without trust are tenuous, directions are doubted, commitment is of convenience, and results are negatively impacted.

CONTROL: As more complex issues arise and more circumstances evolve in multiple directions at once, centralized, hierarchical "control" becomes much harder to achieve or justify. Leaders are empowering talent, enabling them to do their best work by giving more responsibility and latitude.

New leadership styles are more about oversight than orders, promoting initiative rather than giving instruction, relying on empathy to recognize effective ways to influence and manage their teams. Indeed, a "servant leader" mindset is a powerful orientation for serving clients and fully supporting employees.

Mikael Sorensen of Handelsbanken UK exemplifies the coaching style of leadership. "If somebody comes and asks me if I can take a decision on their behalf," he told me, "I say let's have a discussion; they can ask my advice and draw on my experience. But I always encourage them to take the decision themselves."[7] He reinforced how the bank's trust-based culture also "empowers people to take decisions as close to the actual problem as possible." He noted, "In Handelsbanken, we often depict our organizational structure with an arrow going from left to right—with the customer in the forefront, then the branches, then head-office functions. The arrow is horizontal to stress that everyone in the organization is equally important, whether they work in a branch or in a head-office function."

MINDSET: Leaders need a learning attitude or "student mindset" for managing through a significant transformation. You do not have all the answers, and the answers you have cannot get you very far, and that is ok. Empathy helps you listen and learn from others and encourage others to empathize with you and your challenges. The program director of Leadership and Organizational Development at a European-based, multinational investment bank explained how their country heads needed to mentally shift from visionary to agile leaders. During this period of inflection, projecting out three years is seen as brave, resulting in a shift to shorter timeframes and incremental progress to adapt to the significant market changes and challenges.

Leaders at the bank are adjusting to accept "good enough." With a peer coaching culture, they are connecting in small groups to share and solve problems, learning from each other. This "biting off what we can chew" approach was transparently shared in a March 2021 blog post, "Latest Update on the Future of Work at Citi," by the CEO of Citi, Jane Fraser. She wrote, "These are questions we need to answer, and I have no doubt we will. The pandemic has stretched our capacity for innovative thinking, for solving problems."[8]

TRANSPARENCY: As circumstances change, wide sharing of information by leadership becomes critical to ensuring there are no gaps, since people naturally make up data to fill the void. Just think how they feel left in the dark. Frances McLeod found out by quashing negative rumors, "If you don't fill the silences with something meaningful, they will come up with something. Whatever questions are out there, give them an honest, transparent answer."[9] While some people do not easily speak up, Frances recognizes the benefits. "I've got one person in DC and she's absolutely fearless. She is always very happy to ask the difficult question. Some people are going to have a whinge, but you can't shut that channel down."

When you communicate openly about what is going on, you are both reflecting the corporate tenets and making sure people feel included and valued wherever they are working. When the pandemic started, Brian Day, CEO of Fuze, instituted "Ask Me Anything" virtual sessions to help people feel comfortable knowing they were part of a strong community and able to share whatever concerns they had.[10]

With faster response rates across dispersed teams who bear more responsibility, even bolstered by increased transparency and empathy-driven open communication, things can fall through the cracks, with information imperfectly understood or updated data not shared. Paulette Rowe of the Paysafe Group said, "Calling out your moves is important. You can't say to people, 'I will always act this way or I will always do this.' But you can say, 'I am about to change something, I'm about to adjust, or I have new data,' so I try and signal that."[11]

The most effective approach is to over-communicate and be determinedly unambiguous, providing more, rather than less, detail about what needs to be accomplished. Welcoming clarity and contributions from your team and across your company or group helps highlight successes and opportunities, as well as bring issues to the surface, hopefully before they become problems.

WORKFLOW: Over the last twenty years, the nature of work has been changing, becoming more networked than linear, more project-based than individually tasked, and shorter-term in length rather than projectable over years. Each project or program you lead may now be quite different, while having similar characteristics and using the same process or operational building blocks. However, the flow of work through your organization has been evolving significantly. With an empathetic perspective, you can recognize the challenges for employees who are trying to react appropriately to iterations and adjustments without being able to properly identify, define, and monitor all their work components that need logging, (re)assigning, and optimizing.

In April 2020, as Chief Marketing Officer of Workfront, which provides workflow management solutions, Heidi Melin reported clients' feedback at the height of the pandemic's first wave: "This is helping us continue to keep our business going as we've pivoted to a remote workforce," and, "Even though we're not sitting in the same building and room, we're able to leverage a work management platform that keeps us aligned and provides visibility into the work that's going on day to day." She explained, "Those companies are really focused on ensuring they have a system of record for work, and that visibility has become really critical during this timeframe."[12] Getting granular about workflow becomes an empathetic initiative to help your teams adapt and pivot when warranted, improving operational flexibility and resilience.

PROCESS: Leaders used to not have to define "how work worked." Process was long-established and static. But in a much more fluid, dynamic environment with few hard or even clearly delineated boundaries, for your reports and team members—especially from younger cohorts—an empathetic approach means sharing work principles, useful methods, and process options. Operational elements need to be adaptable, and employees can usefully apply their different points of view regarding how to maximize results. Guiding rather than determining their choices, you can help them channel their energies, as well as create clear demarcations at the beginning and end of work periods to prevent blurring and reduce burnouts. When other teams or colleagues from different departments need to be included to devise a new process or participate in a project, if you shepherd cooperation and promote empathetic discussion, team members compromise effectively and achieve optimal results.

SKILLS: Few managers inventory, map, or monitor the skills of their teams or empathize with what people want or need to learn next. When Sean Hinton, Founder and CEO of SkyHive Technologies, was inspired to build his company— to organize the world's workforce to enable the skilling required for a more efficient global economy—and develop Quantum Labor Analysis, he was President at WhiteWater West Industries in 2017. He told me, "We had 500 people at WhiteWater. We knew the jobs we had hired them to do, but we had no idea what they were actually capable of."[13] They deliberated about how "each employee has a unique 'skill DNA,' a collection of skills that they have acquired throughout their work, life, and educational experiences. How could we rapidly and effectively assess and inventory those skill DNAs and apply it to strategic workforce modeling?" He explained further, "The future success of any company will be significantly impacted by how prepared its workforce is, and leaders are now realizing that skills inventorying becomes extremely important."[14]

Now, the skills required to accomplish our daily tasks need updating frequently as new platforms, applications, and channels become popular. Your focus on the current and updated skills inventory in your company, division, or team is paramount, using empathy to match and move people successfully around your organization as well as overcome barriers to reskilling. While institutional knowledge is carrying more weight, internal reskilling is still not gaining enough traction, advised Dom Price of Atlassian, even though it is greatly needed throughout organizations at every level. He voiced specific concerns about those in leadership positions: "Reskilling is going to be a massive side punch for middle-aged white guys like me who think they know all they need to know through to retirement. 'Oh, there's much more stuff I need to learn? I thought I could just carry on doing my job!' But that's not going to happen. It's going to be huge."[15]

CAREERS: Without the worn, self-directing linear tracks of earlier careers, your team members need your proactive and empathetic involvement to inform and guide their skills development so that it is aligned with various possible career pathways. Their vertical, horizontal, and diagonal next steps may be inside your division, elsewhere in the organization, or possibly in another company in your business ecosystem. Younger team members in your group are attracted and retained by your ability to nurture their potential, which means connecting with their point of view, engaging in their skills-development experience, and using empathy to foster broad-based relationships. At the European investment bank, they recognize that while careers start within each country, at some point new growth can happen only across national entities. As a result, leaders must cultivate networks to support their rising employees' further development.

PERFORMANCE: Moving at the new pace of business, consider what each of your reports needs to keep on top of changes happening in the marketplace and around the organization: frequent check-ins. You may already be using other meetings to share news and updates; however, the shift to empathy-infused coaching approaches for leaders and managers formalizes regular mutually beneficial discussions with each of your reports. Fifteen minutes each week can often suffice for ongoing trust- and confidence-building, useful course-correction, sharing tips, gathering strengths and skills intelligence, hearing frontline anecdotes, and conveying executive updates. Testing and refining new approaches or pivots becomes easier, as feedback can be gathered regularly and less formally until a new process element is working effectively. Annual performance reviews are appropriate for compensation assessments and consideration of raises and promotions.

"At first I thought the foot massages during office hours were a bit demanding, but her work performance is outstanding!"

RECOGNITION: Coaching more than commanding yields the best relationships and results, in part because, as a leader, you can encourage and praise while sharing helpful critique. Giving constructive feedback is not straightforward. Practicing empathy is essential for recognizing how your words are being received; what timing, tone, and approach works best with each person; and what the other person is interpreting. If you might benefit from explicit training, it is certainly worthwhile, since your example as a leader greatly influences how your reports manage and give feedback to their teams. At Forensic Risk Alliance, Frances McLeod discovered that in 2021, managers in the United States and United Kingdom were hesitant and sometimes neither broaching difficult conversations nor giving candid feedback about missed promotions. The ensuing confusion detrimentally affected morale and likely also affected talent development and retention.[16]

Empathy helps you tune in to how employees are thinking and reacting to your comments so you can oversee, boost, and reward the accomplishments of your team members. Tailor rewards, where possible, to individuals, since certain employees prefer private recognition over public praise or monetary benefits or vouchers that suit their interests and needs.

RISK APPETITE: At the current pace, evaluating and taking calculated risks is necessary, which may sometimes be nerve-racking. You can mitigate some of the worry you sense is distracting to employees by clarifying what the boundaries and benchmarks of "reasonable risk" are in different areas and relating to particular projects, which are accompanied with support, not penalty. Jeroen de Kempenaer emphasizes the need for good—even empathetic—governance and the importance of leadership giving clear innovation guidance in writing that specifically responds to important questions for each project—"How far is the team allowed to go? How big and deep is the sandbox?"[17]

Detrimental cover-ups are likely otherwise, as well as constrained creativity and risky behavior. The exercise of assessing risk types and levels of uncertainty is also generally useful to share among the group, so everyone understands the operating conditions and challenges that the business is trying to navigate successfully.

MANNER: The cold, imperious leaders of yesterday are becoming less and less effective. Their teams are not responding to dictatorial, unempathetic, unsupportive attitudes and commands. Why? That approach does not fit with the figurehead who listens, encourages, and supports their team tackling the complex goals they are faced with. As a veteran remote leader, at Workfront Heidi Melin developed her preferred combination—an open Google Calendar and Slack—and established an effective virtual habit by actively urging her team to "drop by" if they ever saw she was online and her schedule was not blocked.[18] Presenting yourself as approachable—and being accessible—is important for encouraging even the more reticent folks to reach out. Connecting through multiple channels allows people to use the means they feel most comfortable with, which lowers resistance further.

A corporate veneer keeps you at a distance and prevents your team from connecting with you properly, reducing feelings of trust, safety, and belonging, which affects outcomes. "Servant leadership" is one effective, long-standing, and deeply empathetic approach, more recently applied in the for-profit world, that can provide for the needs of the group in service of the end results. This approach also aligns with the leadership shift from commanding to coaching.

SUPPORT: Individualized attention is paramount for you as a leader and successful manager in the new working environments. If you do not feel well equipped to accomplish this yet, you are certainly not alone! Most people are not naturally good managers without training and attention that is particularly helpful when overseeing distributed teams. Across different work settings, employees' different work styles and preferences are more obvious, benefiting from more finesse by managers to distinguish the type and timing of support that each person needs. They might be extremely self-sufficient, need a series of milestones, or benefit most from a cheerleader to keep them focused and productive.

Being an inclusive, empathetic leader means managing each person on an equitable basis wherever they are working so they have appropriate access to resources, technical support, and training. Your intentional involvement in their career progression is also important. As described in

Chapter 9, managing meetings, project assignments, and even promotions equitably across hybrid and fully remote teams means creating a "location inclusive" mindset, as Sacha Connor described, to ensure those working regularly or wholly remotely are not forgotten or treated less favorably. Resilience and mental health, which benefit greatly from integrating empathy, are new areas for leaders' heightened awareness going forwards. Frances McLeod emphasized, "You can't help someone be resilient if you are not open to understanding how they function and what their sensibilities are."

Do not forget self-care. You cannot lead effectively if you are not taking care of yourself and paying attention to your mental and physical health. You need to be grounded and emotionally calm, with your brain fully engaged. As Jack Elkins, Chief Sidekick at Sidekick Innovation, a sports innovation consultancy, advises, "You want to check you are in a state to be responsive, not reactive, so you are not emotionally swayed or susceptible and operating from 'survival mode.'"[19]

TOOLS: Technology is driving our new dynamic environments by providing us with artificial intelligence and machine-learning capabilities together with more computing and processing power. You can leverage significant advantage if you are gathering, analyzing, and synthesizing—through the lenses of customers' and employees' experiences—timely data that provides your business with critical competitive intelligence.

Embedding core up-to-date digital capabilities is now a requirement technically to deliver and distribute your products or services, discover how they are being received in the marketplace, and determine and track business workflow. Upgraded applications are also critical to interconnect people across your ecosystem, so they can react and respond quickly, and attract and retain your youngest team members, who recognize which tools signal forward-thinking leadership and a business with competitive advantage.

Project management applications can allow unobtrusive supervision, showing individuals' progress without interruptions or inquiries that could undermine progress and confidence. Workflow management tools necessitate critical understanding of processes to enable operational flexibility. Other increasingly important, even essential, applications include asynchronous communications, complementary chat, and calendaring capabilities, with coordinated selection, integration, navigation, and utilization. Your company and unit must be equipped with the technology stack it needs to compete at the pace of business.

MODEL: Whatever you do, walk your talk! This is imperative. Empathy values and skills require dedication—actions, and words, matter. Everyone within your radius of influence will follow your lead or mimic your behavior if you do what you say, showing you *mean*—and believe—what you say. Articulating any new intention, orientation, and process makes a difference to others when they see you do it. They will be encouraged by your example, by your manifested conviction, and by the ensuing results.

Start Somewhere

What if you do not address these issues? Your job is *a lot* harder. Getting the results you want may often feel like squeezing water from a stone. Employee engagement stays low, miscommunications and misunderstandings are high, collaboration is impaired, and conflict is common, with confusion about responsibilities ending with finger-pointing destroying the cohesion of any team. Productivity is severely hampered. Does that sound like one of the teams you know?

I gave a speech to hundreds of software developers at a software company's user conference in 2019. The presentation was about how empathy improves team performance. After my talk, an IT group lead briskly walked up to me with a burning question.

"But, I have ten direct reports!" he said. "How could I deal with all that emotion? It would be too much!" He looked rather panicked and temporarily overwhelmed at the mere thought of having to empathize with every person on his team.

Leading a large group, and clearly very uncomfortable sharing feelings, he needed quick reassurance. "You don't have to engage emotionally with each person every time," I said. "Just start by asking thoughtful questions and listening to their answers about their work, families, needs, and interests. That shows you care and will makes a significant difference."

His shoulders relaxed. He looked relieved and walked away deep in thought about how to infuse his team interactions with empathy.

The more you can focus empathetically in your leadership role on what each person needs and adjust as much as reasonably possible for them individually, while compromising as needed across the group, the more easily you will be able to achieve all your goals and specific objectives.

Empathy Habits

1 **Show up authentically:** Check regularly how people experience you to ensure perceptions match your intentions.

2 **Ask for inputs:** Accelerate development of trust by asking your reports for help and inputs.

3 **Be accessible and approachable:** Share regular daily times you are available and encourage drop-ins to get people comfortable.

4 **Personalize management:** Purposefully apply individual approaches to manage, motivate, and monitor each team member effectively.

5 **Coach (versus command):** Provide brief weekly check-ins to oversee, course-correct, and provide constructive support for each of your reports.

6 **Increase transparency:** Communicate openly to ensure employees feel respected and included wherever they are working.

7 **Tailor recognition:** Reward accomplishments to value contributions and motivate future efforts, customizing to the individual to achieve optimal effect.

15

Teamwork
Improving Group
Outcomes

AM WAS in a major executive committee meeting and was hoping to pass a key resolution. Afterwards, he said that he recognized the moment when the stage was set and the gathered group was ready to hear the punchline of his persuasive argument. He read the faces of the two key influencers in the room, already knowing their points of view. Sam had developed relationships with every committee member so he could understand their general orientation and standpoint on particular issues. He had also found points of connection to help them better relate and see eye to eye.

Now, he could see that these two linchpin participants were considering the new facts he had laid out, and he tuned in to how they were reacting. One seemed somewhat hesitant—Sam knew the CFO had been putting pressure on him behind the scenes. The other was more relaxed—Sam was aware the woman was close to the CEO but had shown herself to be an independent actor on the committee and could generally be relied upon to review data neutrally.

Sam chose his words carefully. He had taken note of words used to describe ideas viewed as solid and positive in previous committee meeting minutes and exchanges. He used conservative hand gestures for emphasis only, as certain participants were rather dour and he had recently learned that they dismissed large gesticulations as theatrical. Sam did not want to undermine himself or distract anyone, just to create the best setting for making a strong case.

Most importantly, his rationale, research, and questions were targeted at people individually around the group, and he directed critical points at each, knowing their concerns and trigger issues to purposefully speak to or avoid. He watched everyone carefully while he spoke and registered the tension fading in people's faces or posture as, in turn, he saw each person become comfortable with their internal decision.

Sam focused on the last undecided committee members—potential resisters—whom he had identified long before this meeting. He had some extra case points to buttress his reasons and bring them around, and he guided the conversation gently, coaxing the positive energy of others around the table. Then, Sam noticed the clock. He had fifteen more minutes and he wanted—well, he needed—a resolution before the time was up.

He knew he must not rush this. Sam had seen one of the last two holdouts push back very hard in another meeting when they had felt pressured. He was pretty tense, but he knew stressful body language would subconsciously affect the group, so he purposefully relaxed his shoulders and sat back a bit. The movement helped him feel better, too.

He encouraged everyone to share any outstanding concerns. Someone asked about a side issue, and Sam did not want to distract them from the main discussion in the remaining time. However, this person had not spoken yet, and everyone certainly needed to be and feel heard. While Sam answered thoughtfully, he noticed a shift in body position out of the corner of his eye. It was the lead opponent, whose stiff upright posture had softened slightly.

Sam turned with an open expression, inviting more discussion, and waited. He got a softball question. The energy had changed. They were on the same team now. With the shift in the atmosphere, the last hesitation evaporated. With the benefit of preparation work, empathetic relationships, and an understanding of each person's concerns, Sam had connected with everyone in the group and shared the information different people needed, framed in the most digestible way for them. He was relieved. I was, too. Sam is a composite of many people's experiences, including my own.

Teaming Up

You may be involved in running project teams every day or are an integral member of one or more. Or you might now sit on high-level committees and management boards. It may have been a while since you were a team member close to customers on the frontline. However, the scenarios are similar: every participant has intelligence, expertise, and experience to contribute, and they bring their own multidimensional, complex human psychological and emotional dynamics, which both help and hinder productive group interactions.

In fact, teamwork has grown dramatically over the last twenty years. For centuries, we have debated and made important decisions by convening committees and board meetings. We have also had regular meetings for departments or members of a subunit. But the preponderance of tasks for decades was individualized, singular work, with specific interdependencies (for example, on production lines). In 1975, the majority of market value was related to physical assets such as factories, equipment, and inventory; for example, for S&P 500 companies it was 83 percent.[1]

Now "The Project Economy Has Arrived" as a global phenomenon, announced *Harvard Business Review* at the end of 2021, citing the steady rise of projects in Germany since 2009 as a percentage of GDP and the fact that in 2019 projects accounted for as much as 41 percent of the total.[2] We are navigating more uncharted territory and dealing with more independent unknowns and, as a result, more complex challenges and tasks requiring project work that needs two or more people. The two-dimensional façades we frequently presented in conference-room gatherings were sufficient when discussion was mostly one-way, coming from department heads disseminating new directives or decisions made from higher hierarchical levels. Little feedback was warranted or welcomed. However, now we are in a very different place.

Multi-person teams are not only common but also convened and disbanded in different combinations and timeframes, as projects are completed and new objectives requiring different resources and skills must be met. Moreover, we need to "bring our whole selves to work," to participate fully in our groups, but we have been used to more distant, formal modes of interaction.

Every person involved now needs to lean in and speak up, actively bringing their different personal context and texture—their backgrounds, disciplines, perspectives, and ideas. We also need everyone's perspectives, different angles, and experiences to develop a variety of solutions to choose from. Moreover, the best results come when the most diverse range of ideas are thrown into the discussion, drawing everyone out and garnering the most valuable contributions.

We also need to absorb and accommodate these new dimensions we are experiencing of each other if we are to communicate and collaborate successfully, since we are not used to dealing with "this much" of each other! We can do this when we are fully inclusive, when we embrace our curiosity to explore others' points of view with open mindsets. This new reality is why empathy is so important—as leaders of teams and among team members. We need to be able to connect more closely, relate, and debate with each other to test, develop, and launch new ideas to advance business goals.

Earlier chapters mostly discussed empathetic paired conversations, assessing exchanges and ensuing reactions. Indeed, much interplay is bi-directional between the two people talking, regardless of how many others may be around. That said, those not speaking may certainly be or feel involved, and any interaction has some effect on each person present, not forgetting others who might be concerned about the topic but unable to participate synchronously.

To optimize interactions among a team or in another group setting, the best approach is human-centric—experiential rather than transactional. As laid out in Chapter 5, outcomes are highly likely to be better when you can prepare thoughtfully, gathering insights first about every group member. Then, develop your preamble, pay attention to all the exchanges, and follow up carefully and conscientiously. In all cases, adopting a long-term perspective, your nurturing of lasting positive relationships is important to build upon for future productive meetings and outcomes. Your initial attention and effort pay off as you establish empathy habits and these actions become second nature. Meanwhile, your understanding about each person builds quickly with every interaction.

Team Players

The dynamics of interactions involving many people is like a human chess game in which you are both a player and a piece. If you are not a chess player, consider any multiplayer strategy game you play, whether another board game, a video game, or a sport, such as football. Every live piece or player—including you—has an agenda and plan for advancing, contributing, or surviving, all of which interplay. The better you understand the players and their potential strategies, the better the game will be played—the more effective your handling of the meeting will be.

Some attendees may even be playing by slightly different versions of the rules. The stronger your corporate culture, with clearly articulated, manifested values, the more likely people are guided by the same rules and standards of behavior and aligned towards achieving the same goals. However, bringing their breadth of diversity to benefit the conversation or brainstorming session, they should still be providing a useful variety of ways to get there.

Every team member's input is important. Every participant's voice needs to be heard. It is imprudent and unempathetic, as well as not inclusive, to focus only on the most vocal or senior team members. Valuable ideas, approaches, and methodologies may come from any member of the team. Keeping your mind open, with an inclusive attitude to team discussion, yields the best overall results.

Adding more people—three-dimensional human beings—into the equation certainly increases the complexity of any interaction. However, empathy equips you to interpret nuances about each person, revealing insights about the manner and content of their typical interactions with you and others. Surely you are able to recall snippets of conversations between particularly friendly or strained relations pairs of your coworkers. Your empathetic understanding helps that intelligence enrich the interwoven fabric of conversation among a group.

Team Dynamics

Being an effective, productive, and participatory member of any team or group takes attention, skill, and practice, and empathy plays a key role. Knowing relevant details about other people working or serving with you gives you strategic benefits. Build your knowledge about each person's histories and experiences, possible blind spots and triggers, previous projects and outcomes, work style and preferences, strengths and weaknesses, and interests and hobbies, especially ones you might have in common.

Sounds too laborious? There is a way to short-circuit this process and share the work. Ray Dalio, founder of Bridgewater, reported to be the best-performing hedge fund manager of all time,[3] explains in his book *Principles* how he uses an ingenious "baseball-card" approach for each Bridgewater employee to share information about themselves internally.[4] Each employee compiles their personal card, which includes key work-related data such as skills, projects worked on, and achievements, and keeps it up to date. Employees share their cards when they start working together to accelerate mutual understanding.

I recommend creating similar shareable summaries that comprise professional data and some personal information, such as hobbies, sports, and other interests. Exchanging this information helps people recognize each other's skills and strengths, easily identify commonalities, sense how the project work will flow, and jumpstart empathetic exchanges.

Harnessing your natural empathy skills, you can discern what each participant brings to a team or committee discussion, interpreting historical group situations and synthesizing your reflections. Empathy skills help you distinguish details and characteristics of people's inter-relationships and allow you to appreciate how individuals' different perspectives, backgrounds, personal contexts, goals, and talents might play out in a group dynamic: Will they mutually inspire, align, reinforce, overlap, or clash? Empathy helps you anticipate how people are likely to react emotionally to each other's particular arguments or words: which ones they find persuasive, soothing, irritating, combative, or frivolous. Even more importantly, empathy is the skill that permits you to recognize triggers that might detonate and derail a productive, communal discussion.

Sometimes, preemptive conversations may be warranted. These chats are *not* to predetermine the conclusion of a team discussion. Such an objective would be undermining, since it would explicitly or implicitly suggest that others' inputs are not worth listening to, and would have a detrimental impact on team engagement. Instead, touching base with certain people beforehand can ensure a productive group interaction, particularly if certain relationships have been less than harmonious in the past.

Without disturbing the flow of the meeting itself, an early conversation can facilitate people's focus on the meeting's objective when everyone has assembled. Differences in opinion or approach can be softened or put aside and the emphasis placed on the significance of the group debate for advancing a substantial business goal—which every participant is aiming for. Then, you have the best chance of everyone turning up online and in person intent to participate productively with a positive mindset!

Team Roles

Whatever your role on the team, committee, or any other type of working group, everyone influences the human interplay, including you and how you interact with and among the others. Since empathizing starts with you, remember to pay attention to how you show up, how much you listen and talk, how easy you are to understand, how even or volatile your emotions are, and how you sound and sit. All these elements affect exchanges with someone else, and here, with the greater complexity of the group dynamic, bringing greater sensitivity to the role you play in the team or specific meeting improves all interactions and outcomes.

Dom Price of Atlassian shared a revelation: "I had been in meetings where I thought my role was to be the agitator, when actually I was expected to be the decision maker—we were at cross purposes. Now team outcomes have gone through the roof, as when we meet they tell me, 'There are three options,' and I ask, 'What do you think?' I've actually stopped being the decision maker because I've helped *them* make decisions."[5] When he now receives a meeting invitation, Dom asks, "What is my role that you are going to hold me accountable for?"

Undoubtedly, you have noticed certain group behaviors and been using empathy in many subtle ways to be effective in managing individual dynamics in multi-person settings. Now, as an executive leader or manager, it is incumbent upon you to bring your learning and understanding explicitly to model and encourage productive interactions among teams you are leading or working with.

As noted in the previous chapter, to stimulate the most productive interactions and conclude with the best results, leadership styles now emphasize oversight and coaching. In a team context, a leader participating silently or being present as a facilitator encourages everyone else to speak before they do. A good facilitator is alert to personality and power dynamics, reading signals and gauging sentiments to recognize how best to massage the conversation, alternately encouraging people to speak more or less. They smooth potentially sticky moments and ensure all topic elements or agenda items are covered. Good facilitators typically have accentuated empathy skills which they proactively engage.

Paulette Rowe of the Paysafe Group often joins a team discussion, participating as a facilitator, and typically encouraging, informing, and enabling decisions.[6] Remote-work expert Laurel Farrer advocates for having facilitators for virtual brainstorming sessions.[7] The person is ideally someone whom all participants feel comfortable sharing with, to encourage full and active participation.

Dom recommends that leaders in a facilitator role consider these questions: Are we are on the right path towards the outcome? Are we going too deep? Do I need to pull us up? Are we staying too high and I need to push this down? "That's the job of a facilitator," he said, "to listen for the signal or for the silence."[8] Without a skilled facilitator, one person can be designated the responsibility of ensuring that every attendee has the opportunity to share their views. Otherwise, software is now available to actively monitor online discussion to check contributions and reasonable talk time for each team attendee, giving alerts that prompt people to adjust their participation levels so the discussion is more inclusive.

Elias Baltassis of BCG noted that in status update meetings, everyone on the team is encouraged, but not pressured, to speak, with the objective of ensuring that everyone's voice is heard and valued.[9] Contributions are in reverse order of seniority so those less experienced are not unduly influenced by their superiors. Pulse surveys that regularly check how people are doing are anonymous, with user-friendly green, yellow, and red indicators. Anonymity and a track record of action if there are too many red responses generates a participation rate over 80 percent. Creating a quick and easy habit of employees sharing information anonymously enables you to find out promptly how people are doing and follow up as needed.

Job titles often do not capture each person's strengths and skills, so tasks may not be assigned based on who would optimally fulfill them. On any new project, certain team members' skills might overlap while certain individual preferences differ. Taking an empathetic approach, you might consider reallocating select work content on a new project among the team to optimize engagement. Consultants at BCG are given the option of changing project assignments every few months. Consider the mutual benefits of encouraging team members to explore other roles and develop new skills.

In addition, within a team, many non-functional roles are frequently noticeable, irrespective of the targets and tasks. For example, someone often sets the pace, someone else creates diversions and provides entertainment, another person is the cheerleader, and one person steps up to do most supporting check-ins. People can lean into their natural proclivities for these roles and enjoy making—and even be rewarded for—additional valued contributions to help the team advance its goals.

Team Protocols

We are "over-meetinged"! Meetings increased from ten to twenty-three hours per week between 1960 and 2017, and 71 percent of US senior managers felt those meetings were unproductive and inefficient.[10] Furthermore, 65 percent said meetings kept them from completing their own work. Zoom burnout during the pandemic can be attributed in part to endless meetings. Team meetings in particular take up too many people's time, attention, and energy. *Please* be sure any team meeting is necessary, especially now that asynchronous communication through chat or other channels is being used effectively to take small matters and details off meeting agendas and reduce meeting numbers and length. You might want to confirm with a teammate about what really needs debating live with others.

The best teamwork is inspired by the best preparation and contemplation about who needs to be in any meeting, supported by a trusting culture where empathetic communication allows everyone to understand that you are respecting their time, rather than excluding them, if they are not invited. Transparent sharing of project milestones, key meeting outcomes, and progress ensures everyone is kept informed and all participants feel part of the process. Rotational assignments for the added task of notetaking in meetings is offset as team members realize the overall decrease in wasted time and energy attending nonessential meetings. Show how productivity tools enable asynchronous gathering of suggestions and inputs and can be used effectively to ensure important data is not overlooked but is debated and incorporated.

At the beginning of every group project or gathering, always allow time for all members of the group to introduce themselves or reconnect. The exchange of pleasantries and personal stories, anecdotes, and updates is vital for stimulating or re-establishing ties and reminding people of their shared points of view and interests. Multi-person collaborations are enhanced when people feel connected, recognize alliances, and have common ground.

A critical part of practicing empathy is stepping back from your judgments and exposing your assumptions. For any prolonged interaction like a project or committee, set explicit ground rules for group work to confirm appropriate behavior and reduce misunderstandings. Different team leads often have very different protocols and practices. Clarity about how any new project will operate and associated expectations greatly increases the chances of achieving the results you want in the most productive way.

A few helpful rules of engagement:

- Regularly refer to high-level objectives to confirm and align a group's sense of purpose.

- Encourage people to listen and build off each other's words and suggestions.

- Avoid dismissive language and counter words (such as "but").

- Show mutual support for ideas generated within the group.

All these behaviors—modeled by you to be mirrored by others—stimulate more creativity and sharing, since no one feels put down and broader-ranging, free-associating inspiration is encouraged—from every person in the group.

In addition, paying attention to team members' signs, picking a good moment to introduce your idea, and constructively discussing another's rebuttal are all good uses of empathy in team dialogue. You can also notice where enthusiastic validation boosts wider acceptance of ideas you support and formulate suitable targeted questions to test ideas you do not. You can increase quality outcomes by ensuring there is sufficient exploration and debate, with moments for uplifting, coaxing, or countering patiently.

Takeaways are essential to bring any teamwork or group meeting to a conclusion. As a key empathetic principle, bringing the discussion to a close with a summary ensures everyone has the same understanding of the meeting, key points debated, outcomes, and next steps, including any outstanding issues that might need to be dealt with at a later date. Each person can be appropriately tasked with deadlines as applicable.

Every group interaction and follow-up is a chance to reinforce and review how well participants connect and communicate to benefit their teamwork. The better they are able to absorb and process differences of opinion, find common ground, and bridge geographic distances, the more productive their conversations and cooperation are and the less distracted they are by conflict.

Software-generated pulse surveys or quick live debriefs can usefully delve into aspects of productivity as well, for surfacing relationship depth and dynamics which greatly influence team exchanges. Recognition and incentive motivations for empathy-related behaviors also heighten awareness of perspective-taking efforts and capacities and how these benefit meeting interactions and outcomes. Optimizing multidimensional multi-person exchanges is increasingly important as our team-based work volume grows.

In the most expansive interpretation of teamwork, everyone in your company and across your ecosystem is a member of the larger team, contributing along and in service of the optimal Customer Journey: creating value for the business, whatever their group, committee, or board role. Every team member's involvement, manner, and interactions matter. Empathy informs and facilitates productive positive team experiences and outcomes.

Empathy Habits

1   **Know the players:** Before any team launch, do your home-work about all the people involved. For ongoing meetings, ensure you have any important updates on team dynamics.

2   **Set ground rules:** Develop relevant protocols for any prolonged group work to ensure everyone understands expected behaviors and practices.

3   **Play the facilitator:** Especially for important meetings, facilitate the discussion and contributions from everyone, refraining from participating as the leader.

4   **Ask open questions:** Practice open-ended questioning to stimulate more sharing and model how compounding, constructive discussion works.

5   **Check emotions:** Delay or pause meetings or group work if anyone needs a few minutes to calm elevated emotional levels.

6   **Withhold judgments:** Count to three, breathe deeply, or trigger any other habit to distance yourself from your judgment or reaction. The focus is on their experience, not yours.

7   **Conclude with clarity:** Wrap up any work with multiple players so everyone is clear what happened and why and what's next. Conduct relevant follow-ups to benefit future teamwork.

Conclusion
Reorienting
Your Ecosphere

EMPATHY WORKS, doesn't it?

Indeed, empathy doesn't just work. It is the essential foundational value, mindset, and skill that you and your company need to work through these liminal times successfully. Shifting orientation of your business ecosphere through an empathetic lens, using the framework of the Customer Journey and Employee Journey, you can now complete the necessary transformation. You can achieve a new, dynamic equilibrium for your business that crucially balances digital integration with a complementary humanistic focus.

You may have come looking for direction and a viable solution to support you through some rocky, uncharted territory. You might have been drawn to the low-key, subtle, and enduring possibilities of interpersonal skills. But, I venture, you got more than you bargained for. You might have been intrigued by how empathy might create competitive advantage, never mind be "the key" to it. You might not have realized the breadth and depth of the transformation we all have to get through.

But now you know.

Now you understand the undeniable human focus of our futures. Now you understand why and how empathy is the critical ingredient. Yes, without empathy, how could you adapt sufficiently for the human-centric new era of work we are now in? Without empathy, how could you be in a strong enough position to make pervasive, coordinated, and integrated changes, working closely together among and between teams, divisions, and companies all along your value chain? Without empathy, how could you connect, understand, convince, and serve your customers well? Without empathy, how could you build a strong, cohesive culture and community that creates the platform for your growth and success? Without empathy, how could you know what it takes to attract, engage, and retain the critical talent you need?

What tipped the scales for you?

- Was it leaning into a couple of different conversations, asking more open questions, and noticing improved interactions?

- Was it listening more actively, noticing more nuances in people's replies that allowed you to answer differently, resulting in unexpectedly positive outcomes?

- Was it becoming more aware of particular signals from team members dealing with burnout or ongoing stressors?

- Were you on a sales call when you realized what a potential buyer was really saying and what they were indicating about their concerns that you could address?

- Did you recognize your greater awareness of a client's experiences after an interaction that alerted you to ways you could help them with a challenge they were facing?

- Did more concentration on the Customer Journey help you align strategies and tactics across a couple of departments, which augmented particular client solutions?

- Did the shifting landscape of these transitional times suddenly come into sharp focus, showing you the magnitude of what we are dealing with?

- Was it greater sensibility to competitors' faltering attempts at new work parameters?

- Was it the emphasis on customers' experiences that elevated your understanding about team members' daily grind, prompting you to focus on the Employee Journey and how better to engage and energize them consistently?

The dawning of a digitized era of business and the parallel and integral new era of work requires a significant, multidimensional, non-incremental shift. Without major adjustments, most enterprises will struggle to respond in a timely manner to new marketplace developments, including customer-driven updates, supply chain disruption and diversification, and component shortage issues. Everyone, eventually, will acknowledge and update their strategies, operations, and working practices.

While extolling all the significant benefits and sustainable growth you can achieve, I am not going to sugarcoat the risks and significant effort required to make it through the transformation successfully, no matter how much empathy you infuse. If you acknowledge and embrace inevitable hiccups, with a grounded and consistent human-focused orientation to guide everyone and channel people's efforts, the overall transformation can succeed. Miscues will be less frequent and missteps will be smaller.

Beyond that, with a systematic long-term approach, empathy benefits you, your customers, your employees, your business—top and bottom lines—and, with coordination and alignment, all parties involved around your ecosphere. Orienting everyone towards the Customer Journey and complementing and coupling this with emphasis on the Employee Journey commits everyone to empathy-infused human-centric focus and behaviors.

Yes, you need to remember to practice your empathy habits—and help your colleagues sustain theirs too—in the way your company treats customers and managers treat their teams, so there is consistency throughout. Yes, do keep ensuring your habits prioritize empathy in how you are crafting, forming, and implementing a new operating framework and an empathetic employee focus, so your company, division, or team can reorient effectively with a human-centric lens *while in motion*. Empathy will mold and steer people's actions and be maintained by thoughtfully refined routines. There are many possible ways forwards from here, with frequently shifting and evolving conditions. Empathy, and the human-emphasis it underscores, infuses everything with vitality and a coherent strategic orientation that energizes your progress and growth.

This rather "messy" liminal zeitgeist can feel unsettling. Messy can be tough, which is another important reason why a human-centric orientation becomes an important, strategic move. Your intention should be focused on capturing and channeling the rather chaotic energy to stimulate your evolutionary steps forwards. Pervasive integration of empathy with congruent employee experiences ensures that a full, productive transformation to new business and work models, methods, and management can be achieved.

Empathy is not just about kindness, but also understanding. Empathy is not just useful, it is essential. Empathy is not just tactical, it is strategic. Empathy has multidimensional effects, applicable in multifaceted ways across your organization and throughout your business ecosystem. Empathy is critical for your organization's future—as a business and as an employer—and for you in all your important roles as a leader, overseer, supporter, coworker, friend, shoulder-to-lean-on, coach, motivator, guide, and cheerleader.

Empathy works to launch you up to another level. Integrated and applied systematically, it is a radical game-changer for everyone involved. Empathy gives you mental and emotional insights and intelligence from which you gain deep-rooted understanding and confidence about the cohesive ecosystem you work with and in.

Empathy is the key, the catalyst, and the essence of your competitive advantage. Empathy works.

Acknowledgments

MY CHILDREN have told me my work on empathy has made me a better mother. I know my work on empathy has made me a better person, so I am eternally grateful to everyone who has contributed and been part of the journey helping make this book happen.

First of all, a huge thank-you to Page Two for believing in my idea and vision and to the super team who supported me throughout the process, starting with Trena White and Rony Ganon, and extending to Chris Brandt, Kendra Ward, Jenny Govier (including some great negotiations about English grammar and spelling!), Taysia Louie, Alison Strobel, and others I did not interact with much or at all, but I know played their part.

Outside Page Two, I am thankful for so many from whom I received great encouragement and enthusiasm about the book, which helped me put as much energy and time into it as I possibly could. These folks include the Top Three Authors' Club—most importantly AJ Harper and Laura Stone—who kept me (virtual) company for months and gave me great advice, support, and feedback. I am grateful to cartoonist Jonathan Brown, who worked with me to inject levity into it all with his delightful illustrations, and to his daughter Thia, who helped make sure we were on point! Many thanks as well to my INSEAD WhatsApp group who read my endless posts about empathy, the guys in my 'hood who kept me sane as I walked around the block with my dogs in between major writing and editing sessions, and my family—my late mother, Lee; Richard; Angela; Tanya; Andrew; Hannah; and William.

I am very grateful to every single person who has helped me understand more, believed in my work and passion, who has taken time to share their insights, stories and solutions, trials and tribulations, challenges and pain as our workplaces evolve, prior to the pandemic and since March 2020. I gained great insights from so many people—some are quoted, while many others also informed my thinking and perspective, as well as those who provoked me, challenged me, countered my arguments, and made me crystallize and clarify what I really meant! Huge thanks to:

Elias Baltassis; Neil Bedwell; Ronit Berkman; Robert Birge; Matthew Bishop; Gary A. Bolles; Matthew Breitfelder; Brian Bresee; Ben Brooks; Jennifer Brown; Cary Bruce; Muriel Clauson; Pip Coburn; Sacha Connor; Jennifer Corriero; Gena Cox; Brian Day; Jack Elkins; Laurel Farrer; Anastasia Fischer; Laura Fitton; Jeremy Fleming; Jen Fox; Charlotte af Geijerstam; Bob Gower; Norman de Greve; Alessandro Hatami; Sean Hinton; Matthias Hollwich; Lee-Sean Huang; Siham Awada Jaafar; Placid Jover; Molly Kellogg; Jeroen de Kempenaer; Frances McLeod; Heidi Melin; Scott Milrad; Francesca, Mark, and Oliver Nelson-Smith; Anna Persin; Jocelyn Phelps; Beth Porter; Dom Price; Ramon Ray; Mark Read; Paul Reid; Paulette Rowe; Scott Schiller; Alex Shootman; Mikael Sorensen; Lee St. John; Docks Sutherland; Iwo Szapar; Rob Tercek; Fiona Thomas; Mark Thornton; the late Alvin Toffler, RIP; Karyn Twaronite; Jey Van-Sharp; Michael Ventura; Laetitia Vitaud; Jeff Wald; Caroline Webb; Maximilian Weiner; and Kimmi Wernli.

And to all those whom I spoke with who are on their journey into and adjusting for this new era of work. It's not easy and it takes time. I empathize.

Notes

INTRODUCTION

1   Stefania Albanesi et al., "Is Job Polarization Holding Back the Labor Market?" *Liberty Street Economics* (blog), Federal Reserve Bank of New York, March 27, 2013, libertystreeteconomics.newyorkfed.org/2013/03/is-job-polarization-holding-back-the-labor-market.

CHAPTER 1: WHY NOW?

1   Alvin Toffler, *The Third Wave* (New York: Bantam Books, 1984), 26.
2   Ibid., 46–60.
3   Ibid., 155, 179, 231, 245–46.
4   "Covid-19 Impact on Internet of Things (IoT) Market," Markets and Markets, 2021, marketsandmarkets.com/Market-Reports/covid-19-impact-on-iot-market-212332561.html.
5   Muriel Clauson and Sophie Wade, "Skills versus Jobs: Talent Mapping, Mobility, and Management in the Future of Work," in *Transforming Work with Sophie Wade* (podcast), March 26, 2021, 39:35, sophiewade.com/podcast/skills-versus-jobs-talent-mapping-mobility-and-management-in-the-future-of-work.
6   Robert Birge, in discussion with the author, May 10, 2021.
7   John Gerzema and Will Johnson, "Harris Poll COVID-19 Survey Wave 79," The Insight newsletter, Harris Poll, August 30, 2021, theharrispoll-8654532.hs-sites.com/the-insight-wave-79.

CHAPTER 2: WHY EMPATHY?

1   Matthias Hollwich, in discussion with the author, September 14, 2021; Matthias Hollwich and Sophie Wade, "The Office of the Future—Shaping a More Human Experience," in *Transforming Work with Sophie Wade* (podcast), October 29, 2021, sophiewade.com/ podcast/the-office-of-the-future-shaping-a-more-human-experience.

2   Suneera Tandon, "Microsoft CEO Satya Nadella's Leadership Mantra Is All about Empathy," Quartz India, November 7, 2017, qz.com/india/1122336/microsoft-ceo-satya-nadellas-leadership -mantra-is-all-about-empathy.

3   Gary A. Bolles, *The Next Rules of Work: The Mindset, Skillset, and Toolset to Lead Your Organization through Uncertainty* (New York: Kogan Page, 2021), 161–62.

4   Denise M. Rousseau et al., "Not So Different After All: A Cross-Discipline View of Trust," *Academy of Management Review* 23, no. 3 (1998): 395, doi.org/10.5465/amr.1998.926617.

5   Bernd Lahno, "On the Emotional Character of Trust," *Ethical Theory and Moral Practice* 4, no. 2 (2001): 171–89, doi.org/10.1023/A:10114 25102875.

6   Sacha Connor and Sophie Wade, "How to Succeed as a Remote Leader: Inclusion, Innovation, & Iteration," in *Transforming Work with Sophie Wade* (podcast), July 23, 2021, 16:32, sophiewade.com/ podcast/how-to-succeed-as-a-remote-leader-inclusion-innovation -iteration.

7   "Redefining Business Success in a Changing World: CEO Survey," PwC, January 2016, 7, pwc.com/gx/en/ceo-survey/2016/landing -page/pwc-19th-annual-global-ceo-survey.pdf.

8   Randy Borum, *The Science of Interpersonal Trust* (University of South Florida Mental Health Law and Policy Faculty Publications, 2010), 13–14, scholarcommons.usf.edu/mhlp_facpub/574.

9   Jeremy Fleming and Sophie Wade, "Shifting Skills and Scope for Growth and Resilience," in *Transforming Work with Sophie Wade* (podcast), October 8, 2021, 7:52 sophiewade.com/podcast/shifting -skills-and-scope-for-growth-and-resilience.

10 "Stress in America: Generation Z," American Psychological Association, October 2018, 4, apa.org/news/press/releases/stress/ 2018/stress-gen-z.pdf.

11 "A Call for Accountability and Action: The Deloitte Global 2021 Millennial and Gen Z Survey," Deloitte, 2021 12, deloitte.com/ content/dam/Deloitte/global/Documents/2021-deloitte-global -millennial-survey-report.pdf.

12 "Stress in America 2020: A National Mental Health Crisis,"
American Psychological Association, October 2020, 5, apa.org/
news/press/releases/stress/2020/sia-mental-health-crisis.pdf.

CHAPTER 3: HOW EMPATHY WORKS

1 Frans de Waal, *The Age of Empathy: Nature's Lessons for a Kinder
Society* (New York: Three Rivers Press, 2010): 209, 205.

2 *Oxford English Dictionary*, s.v. "empathy," from the second edition
(1989), oed.com/oed2/00074155.

3 *Encyclopedia Britannica*, s.v. "Rudolf Hermann Lotze," britannica
.com/biography/Rudolf-Hermann-Lotze.

4 Helen Riess, with Liz Neporent, *The Empathy Effect: Seven
Neuroscience-Based Keys for Transforming the Way We Live, Love,
Work, and Connect across Differences* (Boulder, CO: Sounds True,
2018), 11–30.

5 Borum, *The Science of Interpersonal Trust*, 36.

6 Ibid., 36.

7 Paul J. Zak, "The Neuroscience of Trust," *Harvard Business Review*,
January–February 2017, hbr.org/2017/01/the-neuroscience-of-trust.

8 Stephanie D. Preston and Frans B.M. de Waal, "Empathy: Its
Ultimate and Proximate Bases," *Behavioral and Brain Sciences* 25,
no. 1 (2002): 1–20, doi.org/10.1017/S0140525X02000018.

9 Daniel Goleman, "The Focused Leader," *Harvard Business Review*,
December 2013, hbr.org/2013/12/the-focused-leader.

10 Daniel Goleman, *Emotional Intelligence: Why It Can Matter More
Than IQ* (New York: Bantam Books, 2006), 43.

11 Michael Ventura and Sophie Wade, "Transforming with Empathy:
From Awareness to Application," in *Transforming Work with Sophie
Wade* (podcast), November 20, 2020, 27:09, sophiewade.com/
podcast/transforming-with-empathy-from-awareness-to-application.

12 Goleman, "The Focused Leader."

13 Ventura and Wade, "Transforming with Empathy," 29:18.

14 Caroline Webb, interview by Sophie Wade, LinkedIn Live, August 13,
2020, 8:20, youtube.com/watch?v=FtWqBmZrffY.

15 Ibid., 8:53.

16 Xiao Ma et al., "The Effect of Diaphragmatic Breathing on Attention,
Negative Affect and Stress in Healthy Adults," *Frontiers in Psychology*
8, no. 874 (2017): 8–9, dx.doi.org/10.3389/fpsyg.2017.00874.

CHAPTER 4: EMPATHY STARTS WITH YOU

1   Steven Kessler, *The 5 Personality Patterns: Your Guide to Understanding Yourself and Others and Developing Emotional Maturity* (Richmond, CA: Bodhi Tree Press, 2015), 26–28, 35.

2   *Encyclopedia Britannica*, s.v. "Protestant ethic," britannica.com/topic/Protestant-ethic.

3   "State of the Global Workplace: 2021 Report," Gallup, 2021, gallup.com/workplace/349484/state-of-the-global-workplace.aspx.

4   "Highlights—Global Productivity: Trends, Drivers, and Policies," World Bank Group, 2021, 1, thedocs.worldbank.org/en/doc/52249 1594657655028-0050022020/original/GlobalProductivitybook highlights.pdf.

5   Frances McLeod, in discussion with the author, August 28, 2021.

CHAPTER 5: BUT IT'S ABOUT THEM

1   "Psychological Safety and the Critical Role of Leadership Development," McKinsey & Company, February 11, 2021, 3, mckinsey.com/business-functions/people-and-organizational -performance/our-insights/psychological-safety-and-the-critical-role -of-leadership-development.

2   Placid Jover, in discussion with the author, May 21, 2021.

3   Danielle LaGree et al., "The Effect of Respect: Respectful Communication at Work Drives Resiliency, Engagement, and Job Satisfaction among Early Career Employees," *International Journal of Business Communication* (May 2021): 1, 16–17, doi.org/10.1177/23294884211016529.

4   Elise Gould and Melat Kassa, "Young Workers Hit Hard by the COVID-19 Economy," Economic Policy Institute, October 14, 2020, epi.org/publication/young-workers-covid-recession.

5   "Spain Jobless Rate at 2-½-Year High in Q3," Trading Economics, October 27, 2020, tradingeconomics.com/spain/unemployment-rate.

6   Anna Persin, in discussion with the author, July 29, 2021.

CHAPTER 6: SHOWING EMPATHY WORKS

1   *Encyclopedia Britannica*, s.v. "behavioral science," britannica.com/science/behavioral-science.

2   Norman de Greve and Sophie Wade, "The Integral Role of Empathy in Leadership and Business," in *Transforming Work with Sophie Wade* (podcast), June 26, 2020, 18:31, sophiewade.com/podcast/the-integral-role-of-empathy-in-leadership-and-business.

3   Sophie Wade, "The Secret for Sales Success in the Tech-Driven,
    Evolving Marketplace: Empathy," *Medium*, December 20, 2019,
    sophiewade.medium.com/the-secret-for-sales-success-in-the-tech
    -driven-evolving-marketplace-empathy-f92054fbef93.
4   Mary Barra, "Embracing a New Way of Working," LinkedIn, April 20,
    2021, linkedin.com/pulse/embracing-new-way-working-mary-barra.

CHAPTER 7: INTERVENTION AND INFLECTION

1   Kimmi Wernli and Sophie Wade, "Aligning Values, Collaborating
    in Crisis," in *Transforming Work with Sophie Wade* (podcast),
    May 8, 2020, 25:00, sophiewade.com/podcast/aligning-values
    -collaborating-in-crisis.
2   Ibid., 9:50.
3   "The Rise in Dual Income Households," Pew Research Center,
    June 18, 2015, pewresearch.org/ft_dual-income-households-1960
    -2012-2; Claire Cain Miller and Ernie Tedeschi, "Single Mothers
    Are Surging Into the Work Force," *New York Times*, The Upshot,
    May 29, 2019, nytimes.com/2019/05/29/upshot/single-mothers
    -surge-employment.html.
4   Lauren Weber and Chip Cutter, "A Wake-Up Call for Grads: Entry-
    Level Jobs Aren't So Entry Level Any More," *Wall Street Journal*,
    May 10, 2019, wsj.com/articles/a-wake-up-call-for-grads-entry-level
    -jobs-arent-so-entry-level-any-more-11557480602.
5   *The Ultimate Guide to Generation Z in the Workplace*, InsideOut
    Development, 2019, 8, resources.insideoutdev.com/ebooks/gen-z.
6   Joshua Gotbaum and Bruce Wolfe, "Help People Work Longer
    by Phasing Retirement," Brookings Institution, December 14, 2018,
    brookings.edu/opinions/help-people-work-longer-by-phasing
    -retirement.
7   Caroline Pailliez, "French Pension Reform Talks Deadlocked ahead
    of Nationwide Protests," Reuters, January 10, 2020, reuters.com/
    article/us-france-protests-pensions/french-pension-reform-talks
    -deadlocked-ahead-of-nationwide-protests-idUSKBN1Z915P.
8   "One Year Later: Purpose of a Corporation," Business Roundtable,
    August 2020, purpose.businessroundtable.org.
9   Laetitia Vitaud and Sophie Wade, "The Unbundling and
    Re-bundling of Jobs in the Future of Work," in *Transforming Work
    with Sophie Wade* (podcast), April 23, 2021, 24:09, sophiewade.com/
    podcast/the-unbundling-and-re-bundling-of-jobs-in-the-future
    -of-work.

10 Matthew Bishop and Sophie Wade, "Reforming Capitalism, Promoting Human Capital Strategy, and Embracing the Future of Work," in *Transforming Work with Sophie Wade* (podcast), February 26, 2021, 4:30, sophiewade.com/podcast/reforming -capitalism-promoting-human-capital-strategy-and-embracing-the -future-of-work.

11 de Greve and Wade, "The Integral Role of Empathy in Leadership and Business," 4:45.

12 Neil Bedwell and Sophie Wade, "Marketing Internally to Effect Change, with Empathy," in *Transforming Work with Sophie Wade* (podcast), June 25, 2021, 37:15, sophiewade.com/podcast/marketing -internally-to-effect-change-with-empathy.

13 Clauson and Wade, "Skills versus Jobs," 12:29.

CHAPTER 8: THE HUMAN-CENTRIC SYSTEM

1   de Greve and Wade, "The Integral Role of Empathy in Leadership and Business," 5:19.

2   Deloitte, "2022 Global Marketing Trends: Put Customers First," *Wall Street Journal*, CMO Today, October 27, 2021, deloitte.wsj .com/articles/2022-global-marketing-trends-put-customers-first -01635352161?mod=djemCMOToday.

3   Mikael Sorensen, in discussion with the author, September 8, 2021.

4   Molly Kellogg, in discussion with the author, August 31, 2021.

CHAPTER 9: NEW WORK MODELS

1   Cary Bruce, in discussion with the author, March 11, 2021.

2   Cary Bruce, email message to author, October 18, 2021.

3   "Job Openings and Labor Turnover Summary," Economic News Release, US Bureau of Labor Statistics, October 12, 2021, bls.gov/ news.release/jolts.nr0.htm.

4   Rosalie Chan, "Atlassian Just Told Employees They Can Work from Home Permanently, Following Twitter and Facebook," *Business Insider*, August 7, 2020, businessinsider.com/atlassian-says- employees-they-can-work-from-home-permanently-2020-8?amp.

5   Sahar Nazir, "John Lewis to Allow Flexible Working for All Head Office Staff," *Retail Gazette*, July 6, 2021, retailgazette.co.uk/blog/ 2021/07/john-lewis-to-allow-flexible-working-for-all-head -office-staff.

6   "The Right to Request Flexible Working: An Acas Guide," Acas, June 2014, 2. Accessed via Employment Law Watch, employment lawwatch.com/wp-content/uploads/sites/7/2014/07/The-right-to -request-flexible-working-the-Acas-gui.pdf.

7   Ibid., 3–7.

8   Ricardo Semler, *Maverick: The Success Story behind the World's Most Unusual Workplace* (New York: Grand Central Publishing, 1995), 123, 128.

9   Connor and Wade, "How to Succeed as a Remote Leader," 19:20.

10 Jeroen de Kempenaer, in discussion with the author, July 29, 2021.

11 Laurel Farrer, in discussion with the author, August 11, 2021.

12 Wade, "The Secret for Sales Success in the Tech-Driven, Evolving Marketplace."

13 Sophie Wade, "The Six Secrets of Effective Remote Working and Collaborating," *HuffPost*, December 18, 2017, huffpost.com/entry/ the-six-secrets-of-effective-remote-working-and-collaborating_b_5a3 806dde4b02bd1c8c60904.

14 Connor and Wade, "How to Succeed as a Remote Leader," 13:09.

15 Ibid., 13:55.

CHAPTER 10: CULTURE

1   Jey Van-Sharp and Sophie Wade, "Why Culture Matters— Especially Now," in *Transforming Work with Sophie Wade* (podcast), July 10, 2020, 3:15, sophiewade.com/podcast/why-culture-matters -especially-now.

2   Kellogg, discussion.

3   Sorensen, discussion.

4   Bill Murphy Jr., "Tesla's 'Anti-handbook Handbook' for New Employees Just Leaked. It's Pure Elon Musk, and Your Business Should Definitely Copy It," *Inc.*, February 16, 2020, inc.com/bill -murphy-jr/teslas-anti-handbook-handbook-for-new-employees -just-leaked-its-pure-elon-musk-your-business-should-definitely -copy-it.html.

5   Richard Branson, "Adventure as a Culture," *Richard Branson's Blog*, Virgin, August 23, 2017, virgin.com/branson-family/richard -branson-blog/adventure-culture.

6   Van-Sharp and Wade, "Why Culture Matters," 21:50.

7   Ibid., 9:15.

8   Paul Reid and Sophie Wade, "Triggering Trust and Engagement through Anonymity and Action," in *Transforming Work with Sophie Wade* (podcast), May 28, 2021, 11:07, sophiewade.com/podcast/triggering-trust-and-engagement-through-anonymity-and-action.

9   Dom Price, Work Futurist at Atlassian, email message to author, September 28, 2021.

10   Lauren A. Rivera, "Hiring as Cultural Matching: The Case of Elite Professional Service Firms," *American Sociological Review* 77, no. 6 (2012): 1, 2, 8, doi.org/10.1177/0003122412463213.

11   Karyn Twaronite and Sophie Wade, "Leaning Into Diversity and Inclusiveness with Empathy," in *Transforming Work with Sophie Wade* (podcast), August 28, 2020, 5:24, sophiewade.com/podcast/leaning-into-diversity-and-inclusiveness-with-empathy.

12   Zak, "The Neuroscience of Trust."

13   Reid and Wade, "Triggering Trust and Engagement through Anonymity and Action," 4:00.

14   Zak, "The Neuroscience of Trust."

15   Consuelo H. Wilkins, "Effective Engagement Requires Trust and Being Trustworthy," *Medical Care* 56, no. 10, supplement 1 (2018), dx.doi.org/10.1097%2FMLR.0000000000000953.

16   Zak, "The Neuroscience of Trust."

CHAPTER 11: THE CONTEMPORARY WORKER

1   Zoe Schiffer, "Apple Employees Push Back against Returning to the Office in Internal Letter," *The Verge*, June 4, 2021, theverge.com/2021/6/4/22491629/apple-employees-push-back-return-office-internal-letter-tim-cook.

2   Beth Porter and Sophie Wade, "The Secrets of Productive Remote Meetings," in *Transforming Work with Sophie Wade* (podcast), February 27, 2020, 21:59, sophiewade.com/podcast/the-secrets-of-productive-remote-meetings.

3   Ibid.

4   Ibid., 26:38.

5   Van-Sharp and Wade, "Why Culture Matters," 14:45.

6   Ibid., 21:16.

7   Jennifer Brown, interview by Sophie Wade, LinkedIn Live, September 29, 2020, 25:00, youtube.com/watch?v=GOaJL8ZIrT0.

8   Mark Read and Sophie Wade, "Empathy: At the Core of Corporate Culture," in *Transforming Work with Sophie Wade* (podcast), July 24, 2020, 32:03, sophiewade.com/podcast/empathy-at-the-core-of -corporate-culture.

9   Siham Awada Jaafar and Sophie Wade, "Diversity & Inclusion Are Founded on Empathy," in *Transforming Work with Sophie Wade* (podcast), August 7, 2020, 9:40, sophiewade.com/podcast/diversity -inclusion-are-founded-on-empathy.

10 de Greve and Wade, "The Integral Role of Empathy in Leadership and Business," 23:22.

11 Read and Wade, "Empathy," 31:48.

12 Brown, interview by Wade, 50:26.

13 Van-Sharp and Wade, "Why Culture Matters," 19:05.

14 Jaafar and Wade, "Diversity & Inclusion Are Founded on Empathy," 36:15.

15 de Greve and Wade, "The Integral Role of Empathy in Leadership and Business," 26:45.

16 Gena Cox, interview by Sophie Wade, LinkedIn Live, March 25, 2021, 1:00:44, youtube.com/watch?v=9Yq3-fDHLzU.

17 Ibid., 45:28.

18 Brown, interview by Wade, 26:53.

19 Twaronite and Wade, "Leaning Into Diversity and Inclusiveness with Empathy," 22:09.

20 Read and Wade, "Empathy," 30:53.

21 "Risk of Exposure to COVID-19: Racial and Ethnic Health Disparities," Centers for Disease Control and Prevention, December 10, 2020, cdc.gov/coronavirus/2019-ncov/community/ health-equity/racial-ethnic-disparities/increased-risk-exposure.html.

22 "COVID-19's Impact on Migrant Communities," European Website on Integration, European Commission, updated July 27, 2020, ec.europa.eu/migrant-integration/news/covid-19s-impact-on -migrant-communities.

23 Emily Rauhala et al., "How the Pandemic Set Back Women's Progress in the Global Workforce," *Washington Post*, August 28, 2021, washingtonpost.com/world/interactive/2021/coronavirus -women-work.

CHAPTER 12: EXPERIENTIAL ELEMENTS

1   Paulette Rowe, in discussion with the author, September 10, 2021.

2   Wade, "The Secret for Sales Success in the Tech-Driven, Evolving Marketplace."

3   Reid and Wade, "Triggering Trust and Engagement through Anonymity and Action," 38:25.

4   Brian J. Brim, "How a Focus on People's Strengths Increases Their Work Engagement," Gallup, May 2, 2019, gallup.com/workplace/ 242096/focus-people-strengths-increases-work-engagement.aspx.

5   "Average Spend on Workplace Training per Employee Worldwide from 2008 to 2019," Statista, 2021, statista.com/statistics/738519/ workplace-training-spending-per-employee.

6   John Seely Brown, "Working/Learning/Leading in the Exponential Age," presentation at 2016 AACSB (Association to Advance Collegiate Schools of Business) International Deans Conference, Miami, FL, 8, johnseelybrown.com/WorkingLearningLeading.pdf.

7   Peter F. Drucker, *Management Challenges for the 21st Century* (Oxford: Butterworth-Heinemann, 1999), 142.

8   Oliver Nelson-Smith, in discussion with the author, September 10, 2021.

9   Michael J. Mauboussin, "The True Measures of Success," *Harvard Business Review*, October 2012, hbr.org/2012/10/the-true-measures -of-success.

10 "Labor Productivity and Costs: Frequently Asked Questions," US Bureau of Labor Statistics, bls.gov/lpc/faqs.htm.

11 Drucker, *Management Challenges for the 21st Century*, 142.

12 Dom Price, in discussion with the author, July 29, 2021.

13 Elias Baltassis, in discussion with the author, September 8, 2021.

14 Nelson-Smith, discussion.

15 Brad Shuck and Thomas G. Reio Jr., "Employee Engagement and Well-Being: A Moderation Model and Implications for Practice," *Journal of Leadership & Organizational Studies* 21, no. 1 (2013): 43–44, 54–55, doi.org/10.1177%2F1548051813494240.

16 "Mental Health and Employers: Refreshing the Case for Investment," Deloitte, January 2020, 12, deloitte.com/content/dam/Deloitte/ uk/Documents/consultancy/deloitte-uk-mental-health-and -employers.pdf.

17 "The Other COVID-19 Crisis: Mental Health," Qualtrics, April 14, 2020, qualtrics.com/blog/confronting-mental-health.

18 "2021 Mental Health at Work Report," Mind Share Partners, 2021, 4, mindsharepartners.org/mentalhealthatworkreport-2021.

19 "The Future of Jobs Report 2020," World Economic Forum, October 20, 2020, 5–6, weforum.org/reports/the-future-of-jobs-report-2020.

20 Weber and Cutter, "A Wake-Up Call for Grads."

21 Helen Barrett, "Plan for Five Careers in a Lifetime," *Financial Times*, September 5, 2017, ft.com/content/0151d2fe-868a-11e7-8bb1-5ba57 d47eff7.

22 Gary A. Bolles and Sophie Wade, "Adapting Our Systems and Ourselves for a Reset at Work," in *Transforming Work with Sophie Wade* (podcast), May 22, 2020, 39:22, sophiewade.com/podcast/ adapting-ourselves-and-systems-for-a-reset-at-work.

23 Clauson and Wade, "Skills versus Jobs," 42:09.

CHAPTER 13: SALES

1   Scott Schiller, in discussion with the author, September 9, 2021.

2   Ramon Ray and Sophie Wade, "The Empathy Factor Driving Small Business Success in the New Era of Work," in *Transforming Work with Sophie Wade* (podcast), August 17, 2021, 33:20, sophiewade .com/podcast/the-empathy-factor-driving-small-business-success -in-the-new-era-of-work.

3   Ibid., 16:20.

4   Birge, discussion.

5   Wade, "The Secret for Sales Success in the Tech-Driven, Evolving Marketplace."

6   de Kempenaer, discussion.

7   Birge, discussion.

8   Persin, discussion.

9   Birge, discussion.

10 "The 2021 Sales Enablement Report," HubSpot, 2021, 14, hubspot.com/ sales-enablement-report.

11 Wade, "The Secret for Sales Success in the Tech-Driven, Evolving Marketplace."

12 Ibid.

13 Schiller, discussion.

CHAPTER 14: LEADERSHIP

1   de Greve and Wade, "The Integral Role of Empathy in Leadership and Business," 10:52.

2 "KPMG 2021 CEO Outlook: Plugged-In, People-First, Purpose-Led," KPMG International, 2021, 9, assets.kpmg/content/dam/kpmg/xx/pdf/2021/09/kpmg-2021-ceo-outlook.pdf.

3 Read and Wade, "Empathy," 33:33.

4 "KPMG 2021 CEO Outlook," 16.

5 McLeod, discussion.

6 Zak, "The Neuroscience of Trust."

7 Sorensen, discussion.

8 Jane Fraser, "Latest Update on the Future of Work at Citi," *Citi Blog*, March 24, 2021, blog.citigroup.com/2021/03/latest-update-on-the-future-of-work-at-citi.

9 McLeod, discussion.

10 Brian Day and Sophie Wade, "Leading Remotely and Adapting for What's Ahead," in *Transforming Work with Sophie Wade* (podcast), April 26, 2020, 32:37, sophiewade.com/podcast/leading-remotely-and-adapting-for-whats-ahead-2.

11 Rowe, discussion.

12 Heidi Melin and Sophie Wade, "Managing Remote Teams and Workflow," in *Transforming Work with Sophie Wade* (podcast), April 26, 2020, 6:40, sophiewade.com/podcast/managing-remote-teams-and-workflow.

13 Sean Hinton and Sophie Wade, "Optimizing Skills for Today and Tomorrow," in *Transforming Work with Sophie Wade* (podcast), February 27, 2020, 3:45, flexcelnetwork.com/podcast/optimizing-skills-for-today-and-tomorrow.

14 Sean Hinton, email message to author, September 29, 2021.

15 Price, discussion.

16 McLeod, discussion.

17 de Kempenaer, discussion.

18 Melin and Wade, "Managing Remote Teams and Workflow," 16:00.

19 Jack Elkins, in discussion with the author, September 22, 2021.

CHAPTER 15: TEAMWORK

1 Bill Ribaudo, "SNS Special Letter: The Great (Country) Race: Company Business Models and Country GDP—Opportunity or Threat?" Strategic News Service Global Report on Technology and the Economy 23, no. 29, September 3, 2018, 3, deloitte.com/content/dam/Deloitte/us/Documents/finance/company-business-models-country-gdp-opportunity-or-threat%20.pdf.

2   Antonio Nieto-Rodriguez, "The Project Economy Has Arrived," *Harvard Business Review*, November–December 2021, hbr.org/2021/11/the-project-economy-has-arrived.

3   Harry Robertson, "Ray Dalio's Bridgewater Lost $12.1 Billion in 2020—but He's Still the Best-Performing Hedge Fund Manager of All Time," *Business Insider*, January 25, 2021, markets.businessinsider.com/news/stocks/ray-dalio-bridgewater-hedge-fund-lost-12-billion-2020-2021-1.

4   Ray Dalio, *Principles: Life and Work* (New York: Simon & Schuster, 2017), 75.

5   Price, discussion.

6   Rowe, discussion.

7   Laurel Farrer and Sophie Wade, "Remote & Hybrid Models: Realities, Recommendations, Rewards, & Risks," in *Transforming Work with Sophie Wade* (podcast), September 17, 2021, 9:44, sophiewade.com/podcast/remote-hybrid-models-realities-recommendations-rewards-risks.

8   Price, discussion.

9   Baltassis, discussion.

10 Leslie A. Perlow, Constance Noonan Hadley, and Eunice Eun, "Stop the Meeting Madness," *Harvard Business Review*, July–August 2017, hbr.org/2017/07/stop-the-meeting-madness.

References and Resources

The Future of Jobs, Matthew Bishop
The Next Rules of Work, Gary A. Bolles
Change by Design, Tim Brown
Management Challenges for the 21st Century, Peter Drucker
The Power of Habit, Charles Duhigg
Emotions Revealed, Paul Ekman
Nonverbal Messages, Paul Ekman
Emotional Intelligence, Daniel Goleman
Creative Confidence, Tom and David Kelley
Empathy, Roman Krznaric
Distributed Teams, John O'Duinn
The Empathy Effect, Dr. Helen Riess
Better Than Before, Gretchen Rubin
Theory U, Otto C. Scharmer
Maverick, Ricardo Semler
Done Right, Alex Shootman
Future Shock, Alvin Toffler
The Third Wave, Alvin Toffler
Applied Empathy, Michael Ventura
Du labeur à l'ouvrage, Laetitia Vitaud
Never Split the Difference, Chris Voss
The Age of Empathy, Frans de Waal
Embracing Progress, Sophie Wade
How to Have a Good Day, Caroline Webb

About the Author

SOPHIE WADE is a work futurist, international keynote speaker, and authority on Future-of-Work issues. Her first book, *Embracing Progress: Next Steps for the Future of Work,* has been an executive MBA program textbook and required reading for several management school leadership courses. Sophie is a popular online course instructor with several courses on LinkedIn. Her podcast, *Transforming Work with Sophie Wade,* is highly ranked among business news podcasts in many countries around the world.

Sophie is Founder and Workforce Innovation Specialist at Flexcel Network, a Future-of-Work consultancy. Sophie's executive advisory work and transformative workshops help companies futureproof their work environments and attract, engage, and retain their multigenerational and distributed talent. She helps corporations maximize the benefits and minimize the disruption in their transition to talent-focused new work environments.

Sophie has held senior management, strategy, and finance roles around the world—in Asia, Europe, and the United States—working in media, technology, and venture capital for companies such as Yahoo! and IMG. With a strategy and finance focus for her first career, she assisted entrepreneurs and major corporations in identifying, developing, and executing strategic initiatives; building teams and ventures; and creating partnerships.

She served on the Board of the New York City chapter of the National Association of Women Business Owners (NAWBO) as chapter President from 2015 to 2017 and was a member of NAWBO's Presidents Assembly Steering Committee from 2016 to 2019. She is on the NY Advisory Board of Common Sense Media. Sophie has a BA and an MA from Oxford University and an MBA from international business school INSEAD. Sophie has two children and two dogs. She loves to travel, hike, and dance.

Empower Your Business
with Empathy!

THANK YOU for reading *Empathy Works*. With this human-centric operating framework for your business and an empathetic orientation for your culture and people's mind-sets, you will be able to foster enhanced practice of empathy skills to benefit everyone in your ecosystem.

RESOURCES: Here are more resources to support your company's, department's, or unit's transformation.

Empathy Works worksheets and other materials: empathyworks.online

Empathy Works video courses: empathyworks.learnworlds.com

Articles: sophiewade.com/writing; sophiewade.medium.com

Transforming Work with Sophie Wade podcast: sophiewade.com/podcasts

The Work in Progress Report blog: sophiewade.com/blog

SUPPORT: If you are interested to explore how I might be able to support your company's transformation through live discussion and presentations, here are some options.

Keynote presentations and speaking engagements: sophiewade.com

Executive advisory work and workshops: flexcelnetwork.com

SHARING: I really want this book to make a difference and help people improve working environments and interactions and understand each other better. If you enjoyed *Empathy Works*, I would be most appreciative if you could post a short review on your preferred online retailer's website or reading community to encourage others to learn about and practice more empathy. Thank you so much.

CONNECTING: I would love to hear from you to find out what resonated with you or discover what you found most surprising or useful. Please contact me and let me know.

✉ sophie.wade@flexcelnetwork.com
🐦 @ASophieWade
💼 linkedin.com/in/sophie-wade-380b8/

You can also use this QR code to reach my website, contact me, and share your thoughts.

This book is also available as an audiobook and ebook.